Shattered

into

Beautiful

Jami Smith
Luke 1:45

Shattered
into
Beautiful

Delivering the Brokenhearted from Abortion

Jeannie Smith

WinePressPublishing
Great Books, Defined.

WinePress Publishing (PO Box 428, Enumclaw, WA 98022) functions only as book publisher. As such, the ultimate design, content, editorial accuracy, and views expressed or implied in this work are those of the author.

ISBN 13: 978-1-4141-1764-5
ISBN 10: 1-4141-1764-7
Library of Congress Catalog Card Number: 2010903459

This book is dedicated to my daughter
Abagail, who lives eternally with Jesus and in
the heart and mind of her mother.

Contents

Acknowledgments

THERE ARE SO many of you I would like to recognize, but as I have prayed I have decided to use this space to honor those who helped bring this assignment to completion.

First, I lift not only thanks, but also praise to God Almighty for your faithfulness to my heart and this project. It is only because of you that I am able to accomplish anything. Eternity itself is not enough time to thank you for who you are and what you have done for me. I am speechless at your love and long for it to overflow out of me onto everyone I meet.

To my husband, Carter, thank you for your love, support, and belief in me. Unselfishly you have given your heart and time to this ministry. Repeatedly you have read my work and conquered all my computer nightmares. You are definitely the man behind the scenes. I am a better woman because of you.

To our children, Jasmine and Kross, you are the most amazing kids I have ever known. My life has been truly blessed by your presence. Thank you for allowing me the time and tranquility needed to complete this assignment.

To my sisters on the battlefield. I love serving with you! Elaine Lail, you have been my teacher, cheerleader, and friend. Your words still ring in my ears, "Go for it." Most importantly, I honor the unfailing understanding love and guidance you have given me. Your smile is like sunshine to me. Numerous times your encouragement gave me the strength I needed to carry on.

Dana Russell, I look forward to your hugs every time I walk into your building. Your faith in me has presented challenges you knew I needed, but your guidance, friendship, and accountability have strengthened my walk. Our loving, sacrificial team at Grove is amazing and is surely a reflection of your directorship. I am so glad God placed me there.

To CEO Lenna Neill, Jeannie Stoner, Judy Cooter, and the staff at Piedmont Women's Center, thank you for recognizing my need and giving me opportunities to share my testimony. I praise God for this ministry and for your endless commitment to spread God's Word and save lives.

To my mentor, Debbie Wood, thank you for always seeing my heart through spiritual eyes. Your prayers and

Acknowledgments

friendship, my sister, have grown me, carried me, and uplifted me too many times to speak of. I love you.

To Linda Cochrane, thank you for being obedient to God in writing a Bible study that changed my life. My husband thanks you too.

To Linda Gilden, thank you for your sweet encouragement and wisdom that has indeed equipped me to be a better writer. I call myself blessed to have worked with you throughout this venture.

To Pastor Kelly Stanley, thank you for not only uniting my husband and me as one, but also for your influence. You listened as I shared my passion and you freely gave me opportunities to use my spiritual gifts within our church body. I will never forget your words to me. "With rejection comes commitment, with commitment comes success." Many times these words have empowered me to press on. Southside will always be home. I miss you guys.

Last, but certainly not least, thanks to Winepress Publishing Group. I would choose you all over again. To Athena, thank you for your warmness and obedience to God, and for recognizing a need and taking a chance on a girl like me. Mike, thank you for making this adventure completely painless. You exceeded my expectations as project manager. Finally, big thanks to the graphic design team for the quality job you delivered by expressing the heart of my message in design.

The Spirit of the Lord God is upon me; because the Lord hath anointed me to preach good tidings unto the meek; he hath sent me to bind up the brokenhearted, to proclaim liberty to the captives, and to open the prisons to them that are bound; to proclaim the acceptable year of the Lord, and the day of vengeance of our God; to comfort all who mourn, to give unto them beauty for ashes, the oil of joy for mourning, the garment of praise for the spirit of heaviness; that they may be called trees of righteousness, the planting of the Lord, that he might be glorified.

—Isaiah 61:1-3 KJV

Introduction

CLICK, CLICK, CLICK! I can still hear the sound of my heels touching the floor as I pranced around the house in the pink pumps my granddaddy bought me. He always wanted his little baby doll to have a new pair of shoes. I felt so grown up as I buckled the straps around my ankles. Across the room, my granddaddy proudly smiled at me as I showed off my new shoes. At this particular moment, I was convinced I was a princess and all my dreams were going to come true.

Little girls grow up waiting for the perfect fairy tale to come true. We envision how it will all come about: the perfect girl meeting the perfect boy, then love, marriage, and a happy family. I believe some get their fairy tale, but there are the others. For these others, someone with much greater authority has different plans, plans for a purpose to be fulfilled. I am one of the others.

What you hold in your hands is a special treasure. God divinely orchestrated every part of this story. Long ago, all my dreams were shattered by my unplanned pregnancy. Approaching a crossroad, I made a wrong turn, but God in His grace used it for good. That is why I gratefully answered yes to His invitation to share my personal testimony of a sixteen-year journey of post-abortion pain.

Just the word abortion makes many people uncomfortable, but sadly we live in a world where abortion is legally accepted. Chances are abortion has affected you or someone you know. All around us hearts are broken; lives are destroyed, yet the world wants us to believe there are no real consequences for the choice to abort. Well, step back world. Have I got something to say to you!

I wrote this book to prove that the consequences of abortion are very real. Most importantly, this book was written for the women like me who made the wrong choice to abort. This choice exposed itself as a privilege—given to us so freely. Yet it changed our lives forever. I know where you are. I know where you have been. Please know God is much bigger than any difficulty you may have had. He is eager to restore you and heal you just as he did me. It is time to be delivered. It is God's desire that you see with your eyes, hear with your ears, understand with your heart, convert, and be healed.

Introduction

I wrote this book hoping to save lives. If you are a woman considering abortion, I pray this book reaches you in a mighty way. With every breath in my body, I want to tell you that the anguish and pain you will endure mentally and physically from abortion are far greater than any struggle you could possibly encounter raising a child. I know you are scared and confused, but there are loving individuals ready and willing to walk you through this process. Seek counsel and choose life.

You will discover truth as the pages of this book give insight into Scripture and resources that bring hope, encouragement, and deep healing. The message presented means more to me than anything I have ever written. I open my heart to you in the hope you will leave the past where it belongs, make peace with the present, and walk into a bright future.

This assignment has not been easy, but as I grew closer to God, my heart began to break for the same reasons His heart breaks. I have learned it is about His calling and not our comfort. As I boldly share my story, I am less and less concerned about what others think or how many times I am shunned when I share my ministry. Praise God for that!

It is my prayer and desire to become a friend of understanding as I connect with your heart. I was thirty-five before I accepted God's complete healing that He so graciously extended to me. For years I suffered the consequences of my choice, and if anyone had ever told me I would be sitting here typing these words to you, I would have insisted he or she was crazy. But, my friends, God is good and I can honestly say at this particular moment nothing seems more right.

I would like to invite you into my life and to take a journey with me. From start to finish, I want to share with you what my Healer has done for me and what He can do for you. Once I was captive to my sin, but now the only one I am captive to is the Lord Jesus Christ. He now uses me to spread His truth with sincerity like a sweet perfume. I willingly do so with joy on His behalf, knowing He is leading and watching.

Clearly, you are a letter from Christ showing the result of our ministry among you. This "letter" is written not with pen and ink, but with the Spirit of the living God. It is carved not on tablets of stone, but on human hearts.

—2 Corinthians 3:3 NLT

Chapter 1

The Wasted Years

I OFTEN DREAMT of a perfect family. Lost in my dream, I stared out the window of the school bus. Suddenly, the bus stopped in front of my house. I was eager to get inside and tell my parents about my day. I ran through the front yard with my backpack swinging from side to side, hoping my parents would meet me at the front door. This perfect family I dreamt of never existed. No one met me at the door—only the evidence of a dysfunctional family. Sin in several forms had found its way into my family's life and caused us to be broken and divided. As a result, my parents divorced when I was at an early age and my dad became absent from my life.

My mom worked hard to provide for her children. Unfortunately, the financial demands of being a single parent caused her career to steal most of her time from

1

us. As a result, we did not spend much time together. For years I watched other families function and listened to my friends brag about how they were Daddy's little girl. I didn't understand why my life could not be like theirs. Resentment grew in my heart about the life I had been given.

Thankfully, through this transition, I spent a lot of time with my grandmother. I would not trade one single moment we spent together for all the warm sand on the Carolina beaches. She taught me many things, but the most important was who God was. She taught me how to worship and pray, and I was convinced nobody loved the Lord as she did. I am very thankful for my grandmother's presence in my life because she planted a seed that grew me into the woman Christ wanted me to be.

At that time, even though I had memorized all the books of the Bible, I lacked the true meaning of Christianity. I thought it was all about a list of things I couldn't do. I didn't know how to have a personal and intimate relationship with Christ or how to follow him.

If I'd had an intimate relationship with Christ back then, I'm certain my decisions would have looked differently, but I didn't. Eventually, going to church became something I did mostly because it was expected of me. Soon I found other things to occupy my time on Sundays, and I became engulfed by the world.

By age fifteen, I was experiencing the taste of alcohol and enjoying attention from the opposite sex. I recognized the attention I was getting was filling a need, and I became hungry for more. I did not know it at the time, but I was trying to replace the male companionship missing from my life that should have been filled by my dad.

Through counseling I learned that among teenage females, parental divorce has been associated with lower self-esteem, sexual activity, delinquent behaviors, and more difficulty establishing a gratifying, lasting relationship with the opposite sex. Unfortunately, I experienced all of these and they continued to bring hardship to my life.

As a female, I needed my father to be involved in my life. My desire to be valued as a daughter seemed to be a key element in developing the confidence that I was indeed loved. I turned my pain inward. I felt I was not pretty enough, athletic enough, or smart enough to be loved.

I often heard, "Jeannie, you are so pretty," but it was hard to say thank you because I did not believe I was. I tried out for different sports in school in an attempt to fit in, but could never make a team. Finally, someone let me on the cheerleading squad and I found a temporary place in life.

Studies have shown that many young girls experience an appetite for males following a divorce. Girls need a father in their lives who is attentive and loving. I once heard fatherhood described as a security blanket.

Without this blanket, girls can go astray. They become emotionally dependent on others for the lack of love and the masculine example fathers should have provided.

The need of influence from a father is even greater between the ages of eleven and nineteen as this age group is exposed to our sad culture. During this time a young woman needs to be fulfilled at home and covered with her security blanket so she is not tempted to taste the evils of the world.

I love my family very much, and I am not in any way trying to put blame on them for my choices. My choices were mine alone. Actually, I thank God for my family because it was all part of His plan to shape me into the woman He desired me to be so that I could fulfill my purpose. I share these details only so you as my readers have a good understanding of who I was, and the circumstances that surrounded me that I believe influenced my choices.

The next few years brought more temptation and trouble. I began driving and introduced myself to freedom. My mom lost control and my respect, and there was no one there to help her enforce any discipline. Partying became a way of life for me. During this season, I decided I would take my relationships with boys one step further, and I began having unprotected sex. I thought, *Why not?* I had no fear of any consequences.

My sins continued and by the skin of my teeth, I finally graduated high school and made plans to attend the local community college. That summer, I developed a steady sexual relationship with a specific young man. We spent most of our free time together. Soon summer changed into fall and my first semester in college started.

I was so excited to be opening up a new chapter in my life. College brought so much more freedom than high school. Life was good and my plans were well on their way. They changed quickly when one November morning, sitting in class, I began feeling sick. As the sickness continued and more symptoms appeared, a pregnancy test confirmed what I somehow already knew. I was pregnant.

Once the nightmare had sunk in, I decided to tell my mom. Silence was all I heard as I shared my secret with her. Time went on and the silence continued. I sat wondering how I ever got to this place. I felt alone, frightened, and confused. I was sick all the time and eventually missed so many days of school that I could not finish the semester. I felt deserted by everyone, including my friends. Now, here I was all alone, just me and my half-eaten gallon of cookies-and-cream ice cream. What was I going to do?

I retraced my footsteps and could only come up with one thought. I had wasted so much time and made such a mess of my life, what could I do now? Confusion set in, the unknown overtook me, and fear consumed me. I cried and cried some more. I really did not set out to make things difficult in my life. It just seemed that they were.

I am sure no woman sets out to make her life more difficult. Unfortunately, we are all sinners and make mistakes. I am going to pause a moment from my story to say that if you or someone you know is facing an unplanned pregnancy, it is beneficial to understand the negative emotions surrounding the crisis. The most common are fear and confusion. Fear of telling parents and the father, fear of facing the future with this life-changing situation. Fear of health complications or even abortion. The list could go on and it depends on the circumstances of the individual.

Confusion is often the result of desperation to find relief from the pain and fear of the pregnancy and ultimately will impact the ability to make good decisions. Feelings of worthlessness exist and are mostly seen in individuals who have a poor self-image. A pregnancy can sometimes intensify these feelings because of the deep longing to achieve significance and worth.

There are also the emotions of anger, which could be directed in all directions but particularly toward the ones involved. Joy is sometimes present by nature at the initial knowledge of pregnancy but less commonly seen, and then there is guilt which I like to call the silent killer. Guilt is a dangerous emotion and can be very overwhelming. It is dangerous because it can result in an urgent need for help and a change in order to deny the consequences of behavior.

So, exactly what is it we need when facing this crisis? What is it you can give to someone facing an unplanned pregnancy? How about encouragement, acceptance, geniality, empathy, commitment, and most importantly, a listening ear? Love them as Jesus does! How I wish I could have had all these shared with me in my time of need.

The definition of a crisis pregnancy is one in which the woman perceives the people or circumstances in her life to be so threatening that abortion may be considered as the best way to cope with the situation. The length of time spent in this phase will vary from person to person and will include symptoms of anger, denial, bargaining, depression, and acceptance. It is healthy to go through each of these. It is unhealthy to allow any of them to become a stronghold. Do not be taken captive. The only prisoner you need to be is a prisoner of hope.

Unfortunately, I was taken captive for sixteen years. My unplanned pregnancy caused me to reevaluate my life. Because of the pregnancy I perceived my goals and dreams to be shattered. I saw the mistakes I had made and I wanted to start over, but there was just one problem, my circumstances had not changed. I was still pregnant. This was not the plan I had for my life. This was not the dream I had in mind. I wanted to finish school, I wanted a career, and I wanted my fairy tale.

Chapter 2

The Choice That Led to Shame

A FEW WEEKS went by and I cut off all com-munication with the father of the baby. I blamed him for everything and felt he had gotten me pregnant on purpose in hopes of keeping our relationship together. Anger became a constant companion in my life and pointed a finger at everyone including the father, my parents, and myself. Most of the time the first response to any hurt is anger; it was mine. We are all born with the emotion and if we are not careful, anger can cause bitterness to set in. Anger and bitterness can be very destructive and destroy relationships.

Then along came self-pity and I spent most of my time rolling around in it. I had no desire to walk outside of the house, even for a breath of fresh air. The nightmare of the pregnancy had consumed me, and it was as though my life as I knew it had ended.

One day a friend stopped by. As I shared my burden with her, she said to me, "Why don't you get an abortion? Just call and make an appointment and I will take you there. No one has to know."

Finally, I thought, *someone has told me what to do. Someone has an answer to my fears.* Up till this point, I had not even thought of an abortion. I pondered the thought. A distant family member had an abortion. She seemed okay. If she could do it, I guess I could too. It surely would make my life a whole lot easier. Then I could have the new start I desperately wanted.

The next morning, though still confused, I called a nearby abortion clinic. I inquired about abortion because at this point I was convinced that was all I was doing—just inquiring.

"How far along are you?" the lady asked.

"I think about eight weeks."

"Perfect," the voice on the other end of the phone said. She gave me the cost for the abortion and said, "We will see you next week." There was no other discussion. No counseling was offered. I felt like this was my only option.

Later that evening I called the baby's father. "Can I meet you somewhere? I really need to talk to you."

"Okay. I'll be home for a while. Come on over," he replied.

"I really don't want to talk in the house. When you see me pull up, come on outside. We need to be alone."

As I drove to his house, I rehearsed what I wanted to say. How could I make him understand how I felt? How could I let him know how scared I was?

When I turned into the driveway, he came out of the house and down the steps toward the car. I watched as he pulled the handle of the car door.

"Hey," he said with little emotion. "You doing okay?"

"I'm a mess. I have been so confused. I didn't know the right thing to do about the baby. But I have made a decision. The other day Sarah and I were talking. She suggested an abortion."

The baby's father raised one eyebrow.

"I have decided to do that, have an abortion. I think it is the best for both of us. Once this is over we can both get on with our lives."

"An abortion? It may be what *you* think is best, but not me. I really don't think you should do that to our baby," he replied.

"It doesn't matter what you think. It is my body. I will be the one whose life will change forever. This pregnancy was a mistake. You are a nice guy and I care for you, but I don't love you. We need to go our separate ways. That can only happen if I have an abortion. I am scared and I need you to help me."

"What can I do?" he replied.

"I don't have the money for the abortion. I need money."

The baby's father hung his head and replied, "Okay. I will help you, Jeannie. I will give you the money next week when I get paid. But I still don't think you should do this."

I didn't care what he wanted. I never considered how he felt. All I wanted from him was the money to end this nightmare for me. I was functioning out of fear and anger. Reflecting back, I think how his heart must have broken as he handed me the envelope of money to take the life of his baby. I don't know how my decision affected his life, but I pray that his soul is well.

That week seemed to be the longest week of my life as I awaited my appointment. I rehashed everything in my mind, but always came to the same conclusion: I couldn't raise a child. Most of my emotions were negative. Desperation to find relief from the painful circumstances of my unplanned pregnancy produced confusion, and as a result, impacted my decisions.

I thought about the embarrassment the pregnancy would bring to my family, especially to my mom. I didn't want my mistake to reflect on her as a single parent. I knew she had done the best she could do. She had gotten pregnant at eighteen with me, then walked through an unhappy marriage that ended in divorce, and was now living a lonely life struggling to provide.

I felt my decision was the best for everyone involved. As my appointment drew closer, communication continued to be limited between me and my mom. I shared my decision with her, but there was no response. I am convinced she handled it the best way she could at the time. She was just as scared as I was.

The day finally came and there was a knock at the door. My friend was ready to drive me to my appointment, so I grabbed my coat and crawled into her car. I don't remember much about the drive except that it seemed to last forever. Our journey was silent. The only thing I can recall is that I was rocking myself back and forth in the passenger seat. As a child, rocking had brought me comfort.

We pulled into the parking lot, and as I got out of the car, I couldn't help but notice the sky. It looked so gray and gloomy. It was such a cold day as I made my way to the door of the clinic to check in. The inside of the building matched the cold, brisk air outside. I felt so alone and wanted someone to scoop me up and get me out of there. The warm personal touch I longed for was absent. I was scared to death.

Once checked in, I was placed in a waiting room with several other girls all looking to be about my age. My eyes scanned the room and I saw posters surrounding me on the walls that read: "It is your right to choose." Videos assured me I was making the right decision. I looked around the room again, not even able to make eye contact with the other girls. The shame began to build.

The extended wait went on for eternity, and finally the door cracked open and one of the staff members called my name. "Jeannie." I slowly stood and she said, "Come this way." She led me down a long hallway and into a freezing cold room. I felt as if I was on another planet as the nurse came in and handed me a gown.

"Put this on. Do you need something to help you relax?"

"No, thank you," I replied.

"The doctor will be here in a moment." The door slammed behind her.

I sat there shaking until the door finally reopened. The physician came in. His face had no expression. "Lie down, please." I was scared and I looked at the nurse, hoping for some comfort.

"Do what he tells you. This will all be over soon," she said.

I pressed my back into the cold table. I had put all my trust in individuals (whom I can't even describe today) to take care of what I thought was a problem. I had no idea what they were going to do to me physically or if it would harm me. They told me it was just a mass of tissue in my uterus, and at this stage had not yet formed into a baby. I believed what I was told. Unfortunately, I became a victim of Satan's trap because of my ignorance.

I don't remember anything else about my time in that room except for the sound. The distinctive hum of a low-key vacuum was detaching the life God had originated (Genesis 1:26-27) and the life He had fashioned together from the earliest days in my womb (Psalms 139:15-17). Internally I was screaming STOP! But I knew it was too late.

As I listened to the sound of the procedure, I slowly rolled my head to the left only to feel a tear of pain trickle down my face. I was eighteen at the time of my abortion. Little did I know that one tear would remain with me the rest of my life. It would cause years of pain, an unhappy life filled with shame, and guilt that eventually caused a heart of stone.

After it was over, the nurse gave me some discharge instructions and sent me to check out. The first thing I felt was relief, but as I walked back to the lobby, emptiness poured over me. I knew I had made a mistake. *Oh my God! What have I done?* My friend sat there in the lobby ready to take me home.

When I got home, I found myself alone again. I began crying—sobbing. I felt disoriented. It all felt like a nightmare and I wanted to wake up, except I couldn't because it was real. The intensity of the emotional shock I was encountering was a surprise to me. Why didn't they tell me about this? How can this so-called "right" I have as a woman hurt so much? I wondered if the girls with me in that building were now home as I was and feeling the same way. Why didn't they prepare me for this reaction and these emotions?

When my mom arrived home from work, again there was silence. Finally she said, "I wish I would have stopped you from doing it." We never shared any other feelings with one another. Maybe we were scared to hear what the other had to say. One thing I was sure of was that I was going to do whatever I could to forget this had ever happened to me. I did not want to live with this agony every day. I had to forget it and move on. The only way I knew to achieve freedom from the agony was to erase the abortion from my mind and to carry on with life as normal. So beginning the very next day, that is exactly what I did.

Not all women recovering from abortion are affected in the same manner I was. Some have no regrets and can go years without emotional side effects. Some may even advocate in the defense of their decision because of their own circumstances. However, I believe there is some degree of healing needed for every woman who chooses abortion.

We were not created by God to end life. It is His to end because He first gave it. So at some point, we will have to answer to ending a life, and whether we admit it or not, somewhere down deep there is some extent of remorse and a need for healing.

During my research on the effect of abortion on women, I discovered similar stories like my own. Most all regretted their decisions, wanted to encourage women not to consider abortion as an option, and sadly are still suffering the consequences. One woman shares her story:

> After my abortion, I cried hysterically. The nurse said, "Why are you crying? You got what you wanted. Now be quiet. You're going to worry the other girls." I had to be carried to the car and I cried all the way home. I had never felt so much pain as I did that day. It has been four months now, and it still hurts like it was yesterday. I've had no one to talk to who could really understand. I still don't. I live with emptiness in my heart and eyes.

She continues:

> To anyone who is considering abortion, talk to someone first, because you have no idea what you're getting yourself into mentally and emotionally. When I think back to that day when I was sitting alone in the clinic, I wish I'd had the strength to walk out.

Two facts in her story break my heart but are indeed reality. First, the insensitivity the nurse showed her, and second, she still has no one to talk to who understands her. She continues to live with emptiness. This young woman still lives with her pain and has not received healing. Maybe she does not know how to receive healing. This is what inspired me to write this book. Hers is just one voice out of millions crying out for help.

It is my desire for God's healing to reach everyone and for shame over an abortion to become a thing of the past. My choice to abort locked me in a prison of shame; I felt there was no way to escape. I can easily relate to a prison vision. A prison is a place of confinement for someone who has been convicted of a crime. It is a state of captivity. Satan had convinced me this is where I belonged and that I would never get out—in fact, that I didn't deserve to get out. My identity was gone and my shame had put up a roadblock between me and my Lord.

Here is the good news. We are *not* our sins. We are who God says we are; His children. This means we are forgivable, lovable, and, praise God, redeemable. So how do you become a child of God? First, you must confess your sins and your need for Christ. You also have to be willing to turn away from your sins. It is sin that causes separation from God. "For all have sinned, and come short of the glory of God" (Romans 3:23 NLT). You must believe in Him and believe He can do what He says He can.

If you don't know Jesus as your Lord and Savior, I invite you to simply pray this prayer:

Dear Lord Jesus,

I acknowledge that I am a sinner. I humbly ask for your forgiveness. I believe with all my heart that you died for my sins and God raised you from the dead (see Romans 10:9.) At this moment, I turn away from my sins and invite you to come into my life and rule over my heart. I will follow you.

In your name, amen.

The next thing you must do is to overcome your shame. Shame is the result of sin. You have to accept that which cannot be changed. God can take all things and work them for good for those who love Him (see Romans 8:28). He can take our shame and failures and redirect the outcomes for His glory and our successes. I am living proof. No sin, including abortion, is too big for God to handle.

In the first chapter I shared with you all the negative emotions a woman encounters when facing an unplanned pregnancy. Now I want to suggest you turn negativity into hope. Keep an attitude that allows God to work through you. He can only work where there is faith, and you must have hope before you can have faith. Be a prisoner of hope, and accept what Jesus died to give you.

So, what happens when women walk in faith? God takes them to extraordinary places.

Chapter 3

The Lonely Aches

AFTER MY ABORTION, I attempted to bury my grief, turn my emotions off, and move on. I did not return to school right away. Instead, I decided to go to work full time and earn an income. I spent time with my friends and made every effort to keep myself busy. It was as though I was constantly running from something . . . maybe God. There was a constant battle in my mind. When reminders surfaced, I quickly rationalized why I was better off without a child in my life. I was determined to justify the abortion by pressing forth and achieving all the goals I thought I could not reach if my pregnancy had continued.

My weekends were filled with parties, occasionally drugs, and alcohol. Surprisingly, my intake of these toxins did not increase after my abortion, but actually decreased. However, I still continued. Soon, through acquaintances, I met my first love and began my first long relationship.

We spent all our time outside of work together and eventually my friends and the partying lifestyle I had chosen became a thing of the past. I was not giving up this guy for anything or anyone. He made me feel very special and loved. I am convinced that is why I fell in love with him. He gave me something I had never experienced before from a masculine figure and it felt good.

I became very close to his family and spent more time at his house than at my own. Over time, I felt as though I belonged and soon found myself not even wanting to go home. After all, my mom was still working a lot and my brother had started driving and was never there. Going home just meant walking into an empty house. As a result, the relationship progressed and I began packing a bag to sleep over. The slumber parties eventually led to the two of us deciding we wanted to live together. One sin led to the next.

My change of interests had consumed me. I filled my time and emptiness with my new love and the abortion became a thing of the past—or at least I thought so. I was in denial and looking forward to a new future. I constantly struggled to turn off my emotions connected to the abortion. I told myself to forget about it. I was going to get my fairy tale. What I didn't realize was that abortion had relieved me only temporarily of my fears. A whole new set of burdens were soon to come.

I became dependent on a relationship that was not good for me. My boyfriend had allowed drugs to enter his life. The trust I had once had was gone and most of the time I felt as if I were living in a nightmare. I continued to stay and convinced myself I needed him. Really, I was just scared to lose another male companion in my life.

This relationship lasted a little over three years. During that time my self-image was destroyed even more. I felt unworthy. I felt this was as good as it would get for someone who had made the choices I had made. Distortion set in. It was hard to look at myself in the mirror. The relationship brought rejection, hurt, and selfishness. When the unhappiness became more than I could bear, I decided to leave and move back home.

Things changed a little during the few years I had been away from home, so I came back to a different environment. Following in my footsteps, my brother had moved out. Mom had met a nice God-loving man and within a few weeks decided to get married. I now had a stepfather and a new stepbrother. Although it was quite an adjustment, having a man back in our home eventually helped me tremendously.

I continued to work. I was still in the process of mending my heart from the last relationship when I was introduced to a really nice guy through friends at work.

It wasn't long before our friendship blossomed into an intimate relationship. He was so different than any guy I had ever been exposed to and my family loved him. He really was the perfect guy, which motivated me to stay with him for the next couple of years.

As much as I wanted it, the emotional attachment was not there for me. I cared for him deeply, but never seem to fall in love with him. Maybe I thought he was just too nice a guy and I did not deserve him. Whatever the reason, I did not think it was fair to him to allow the relationship to carry on, so I ended it. No one really knew the real me. If this nice guy had known the truth he probably would not have wanted me. I was continuing to hide my secret from family, friends, boyfriends, and even doctors.

After the break-up, I returned to the single life with my friends and eventually met another guy. Do you see the pattern? It was one guy after another. I was searching for something, trying to fill the emptiness in my life. I did not know how to be alone and I did not want to be alone. I needed an emotional attachment to something good or bad, and that is just what the next several relationships were—bad.

The relationships were always lengthy and unhealthy. I was taken advantage of, rejected, lied to, and basically stomped all over. And I took it. The pattern was that I chose to go from one relationship to the next trying to keep a male in my life and clinging to all the bad ones.

It was as if the worse they treated me, the more I wanted them. Because I allowed this to go on, my self-image was shattered.

If only I had known Psalm 68:5-6, which tells us that God is the father to the fatherless. He sets the solitary in families and brings out those which are bound with chains. If I had known this truth, I would have not been trying so hard to fulfill something I thought I did not have. Instead, I kept men in my life to replace my father, and I settled for disrespect because I felt that was all I was worth because of my sin.

My relationships always came to an ugly end. Eventually the scenery left a bad taste in my mouth. It became too much of a reminder of my past and my mistakes. It was not working for me anymore. I felt I needed to run farther. I needed to get out of town and go where no one knew me and start over.

I shared my decision with my mom and stepdad. They agreed this was most likely a good choice for me. They prayed for me and supported me as I tried to switch gears in my life. I started spending more time at home, and I was really enjoying the influence of my stepdad. It was as if I had a family again, and I was experiencing what it was like to have a normal, happy home. I am convinced that some of the better choices of my life were the result of my stepdad's presence. Thank God for good stepparents.

As I continued to work, I reenrolled in the community college, chose a career, and put all my focus on my studies. I picked up another job on the weekends for extra cash so I could pay my bills and save money for school. My hard work paid off, and my good grades coasted me into the college and program I wanted. My family was proud of me, and for the first time ever I felt a real sense of accomplishment.

The college was a couple of hours away from home, and that was far enough so that no one would know me while being close enough that I could easily come home if I wanted. So for the next several weeks, I prepared. Soon I was on my way. I managed to find an apartment close to my school and a job that would pay my bills. I was as happy as I could temporarily be.

Soon I became involved in another relationship. I know. Here we go again, and believe me, this one was no better than the others. Matter of fact, it was worse because I dated him all through college, and in the end he was unfaithful to me. I was so depressed that even with all the pain he caused me, I still tried to hang onto him.

Good grief! What was my problem? I look back now and I think what a sad puppy I was. I remember my brother asking me, "Why do you keep dating these losers?"

He said, "You could have so much better." I could not give him an answer because I rightly did not know. *Something must be wrong with me*, I thought, and for the next several weeks or months, I was just plain miserable. Then one day I snapped out of it.

That was it! I'd had it! I made a vow to myself to stay single. I mean, obviously, dating was not my thing. I was doing just fine in every category but relationships, and I decided I needed to focus more on my successes. I graduated with honors, got my degree, and passed the licensure board of physical therapy. I had already been given a job offer before I graduated so I was able to begin work right away.

I bought my first car and first home and was so proud of myself. Emotionally, however, I was still a mess. I knew there had to be more to life than what I was experiencing. There had to be someone to bring me joy, fill my emptiness, and satisfy my soul. Then, suddenly, I remembered there *was* Someone who could do all these things, and His name was Jesus. Only He could give me the love I so desperately craved and needed. Only He would never leave me or forsake me (see Hebrews 13:5).

Bells started ringing in my head as I quickly leaped up and ran upstairs to locate my Bible. There it was on the shelf, right where I had so long ago left it when I had unpacked. As my fingertips reached out for it, memory after memory resurfaced in my mind, reminding me of the lessons my grandmother had taught me. As I walked back downstairs in slow motion, I thought, *What have I been doing all these years?* I had been running from the one Person who could help me.

It was in that moment in the quietness of my home that I sat in the center of my living room floor and cried out to God. I asked Him to forgive me of my sins and to come into my life, and I knew at that moment He did. In spite of my mistakes, God loved me for whom He had created me to be. That night He met me just the way I was. He knew everything about me—my hopes, fears, and dreams. He had been with me the day of my abortion even though I thought I was alone. He was there, and He had always been there. All that time I had spent running, He had followed me, just waiting for me to turn around and face Him with open arms.

Tears streamed down my face as I reflected on my life. My deep longings to achieve some sort of importance or significance was what led me to an unplanned pregnancy. My choice to abort just added more worthlessness to the image I saw in the mirror. As a result, I had spent years in bad relationships, tolerating the intolerable and living with depression and bitterness, all because I suffered from a poor self-image.

There was a poem written in 2002 by Ailsa Yates titled "Self Image." It was written only one year earlier than the night when I decided to walk with Christ. Praise God for the writer because she was able to capture what my heart was screaming during this season of my life. Here is what it read:

Self Image

I call you, Lord,
And shy away, from all you have to give;
I dare to call you Father,
And my spirit starts to live.
I can't conceive a Lordly One
Could ever care for me,
Or that the One, who rules the world
Would die to set me free.
Yet when I call you Father
And allow your love to flow;
Then all your might and majesty,
You gently to me show.
You ask that I should trust you,
A simple task it would seem;
Yet love I once was sure of,
Seems but a distant dream.
Why should it be so hard a task?
To hold this love you've shown?
To simply bring to memory
The promises I've known.
It seems a poor excuse,
One I've no right to spout,
To say that all my hope and trust,
Has been replaced by doubt.
I do not doubt that God exists,
And rules over land and sea;
But that this Lord Almighty
Should truly care for me.

A doubt that is quite unfounded,
As I daily tend my tasks;
And find that God is always there,
To help me when I ask.
His love is not condemning,
Though often I let Him down,
Yet if I look, His smile I see,
Not some expected frown.
His patience is longsuffering,
And long He suffers me;
For all my fears and doubting,
His love won't cease to be.
His love is never ending,
He pours it from above,
And soaks this hurting child of His,
In His cleansing, healing love.
No more I'll doubt nor stumble,
A claim I long to make;
But 'tis only wishful thinking,
Such promises I'd break.
But trusting in His goodness,
I'll edge ever slowly forward,
And try to place my doubts and fears,
In the strong hands of my Lord.

—Ailsa Yates

Amen! Amen! This is where it really starts to get good. Even today those words bring tears to my eyes. My heart just smiles as I can still feel God embrace me with His hug every time I read the words. Oh, I hope you can feel Him too. If in any way you suffer from poor self-image, stop right now. Go back and slowly read the poem again. Meditate on the words and let God's truth soak into your mind and heart.

I was so excited about what happened that night in my home. It was a divine appointment with just me and the Lord . . . and I was saved. Peace filled my heart and poured over me. Interestingly enough, I didn't think much about the abortion that night other than that I knew God had forgiven me. I was too focused on my new love affair. I knew I had finally found the One who would never hurt me or forsake me. That night I slept the best I had slept in years. I am certain some of the laugh lines around my mouth today are from the constant smile I kept through that night. I surely hope so.

Chapter 4

The Unfulfilled Healing

M Y NEW LOVE affair with God ignited a fire down in my soul. I was eager to learn everything I could about Him. The next day I made my way to the Christian bookstore to purchase a Bible. So many great choices! As I ran my fingers across different versions, I was drawn to a beautiful, shiny black cover. On the inside it read, "The grass withereth, the flower fadeth: but the word of our God shall stand for ever" (Isaiah 40:8 KJV). The search was over. I bought myself a gift that accompanies me everywhere I go, and I always know where it is. I am referring to the gift of God's Word.

I became obsessed with my journey to truth. I knew there was much more to this awesome God than I remembered as a child. My new evening love affair with God and Milk Duds was bringing me great contentment.

Then one day at work my friend said, "Jeannie, there is someone I want you to meet."

Oh no! Not again. Another broken relationship was the last thing I needed.

"Here he comes," she said. "His name is Carter."

I looked up, and he was walking down the hall towards us. I had to admit he was gorgeous. *Even more reason to stay away from him. He has to be trouble.*

Carter was a nurse. I was a therapist, and opportunity landed us on the same floor of the hospital where we worked together. Our coworkers and even our patients wanted to see us together as a couple. However, I was not interested. I had built a stone wall around my heart and no one was going to tear it down. The more he winked at me, the more I avoided him. Then one day he approached me and asked, "Will you go out with me?"

"No, thanks," I answered.

I'm chuckling as I remember this day because the expression he held on his face was a sure giveaway no one had ever turned him down. I didn't think Carter was my type. I learned he had been married before and had two children. I honestly did not want to get involved, but as time went on and we became friends, there was just something about him I could not shake. When the question arose again, "Will you go out with me?" curiosity got the best of me and I gave in and agreed to go.

After hours of talking and one date leading to another, Carter and I quickly fell in love. Before we knew it, we were exploring the topic of marriage. He introduced me to his children and his family, and I instantly formed a bond with them. It was wonderful for a while, but soon our individual fears of relationship caused us to stay apart as much as it caused us to be together. He was afraid of another broken marriage and I was afraid of the unknown.

Looking back on the situation, I realize that my fear was of becoming a mother in a blended family. It was not the plan I had for my life. With all of our insecurities, the one thing we had in common was our faith. We both loved God. So as we took time apart to seek Him about our relationship, we also sought Him individually. God was pursuing us in dissimilar ways. As we traveled different paths, God was busy molding us individually into who He wanted us to be.

I continued to grow in the knowledge of God. I wanted to be baptized while surrounded by my family in the church I had attended as a child. I made the arrangements and traveled to my hometown for the service. It was a glorious day as I prepared my heart and mind to proclaim I was a child of God. As I stood in the baptism pool, I listened to a beautiful song my uncle played for me, and I reflected again back on my life and all my mistakes.

I was so thankful God loved me enough to extend His grace and cleanse me from my sins. Finally, the pastor said, "I baptize you in the name of the Father and of the Son and of the Holy Spirit," but as he lowered me into the pool, the one sin I could not shake was the abortion. I knew God had forgiven me, but perhaps I couldn't forgive myself. My unborn baby was all I could think about as my head hit the water.

After the celebration I traveled back home and it was life as normal. Carter and I continued to stay in touch as we tried to make sense of our lives. Week after week I bounced around, visiting several different churches, and then finally God answered my prayer and placed me right where I belonged. As I continued to grow in my knowledge of God, I couldn't help but think of Carter and the children. Our turbulent relationship had lasted more than two years and even though we tried to date others, our hearts always longed for each other.

One beautiful evening while driving home from work, I found myself content with the Eastern Carolina moist breeze blowing in my windows. My mind shifted to Carter just as my cell phone rang. As I reached to answer, I hoped it was him.

"Hello."

"Hey, Jeannie, how are you?" he asked.

"I am okay, how are you?"

"I miss you terribly. No matter how hard I try, I can't get you off my mind. I love you, Jeannie."

His words made my heart skip a beat. With tears in my eyes I replied, "I love you too."

"Can we meet somewhere and talk?" he asked.

"Sure, I would like that."

The Unfulfilled Healing

Once we met, our hearts joined again like magnets. A month later we were engaged, and six months later we were married. I was an instant wife and mother to two amazing children. Struggles came in all forms, but with God's help we prevailed. My relationship with my husband played a vital part in my recovery from abortion. God knew what He was doing. He placed the right man in my path to meet my needs—a man of courage and compassion. This is the path God chose for me. This is only my story. A woman does not have to find love outside of God for recovery. Jesus Christ is the only groom you need. He alone restores you.

In the beginning of my marriage, I spent a lot of time journaling during my quiet time with God, seeking His direction. There are not many times when I journal that God does not show up at the tip of my pen. He gave me a passion for words, and by putting words into action I am able to look back at His footprints on my life. When the dynamics of my marriage became difficult, God's words guided me through.

While I loved my new family, I was eager to have a child of my own. Through the years I had tried desperately to fill the empty void left by my aborted baby with other things. Nothing worked. I was convinced that if I could only get pregnant and have a baby it would replace the one I had lost and the pain would go away. Carter just wanted to make me happy, so he agreed, and within the first year of marriage we began trying to conceive.

Month after month went by and we were not successful. During this time, Carter discovered the true scars of my abortion. My desire for a child caused me to face my abortion. I thought about my unborn baby more than ever. I started wondering if the abortion had physically damaged me in some way so that I could not conceive. I had to find out, so I made an appointment to see my doctor. How was I going to explain this to her?

Year after year I had denied my pregnancy because I was too ashamed of my abortion. Now, in my doctor's office, I explained and waited for the daggering eyes to look down on me. They never did. Instead, she assured me that physically I was fine and there was no reason why Carter and I could not conceive naturally.

On the way home from the doctor's office, Satan tricked me into believing I was infertile and it was my punishment for choosing to abort. I did everything I could to keep myself busy, but while lying in bed at the end of every day, I stared at the ceiling, consumed with thoughts about my unborn baby. I wondered what he or she would have looked like, what talents he or she would have had. It was torture, to say the least.

I stayed active at church serving and taking Bible study after Bible study, and although I was developing more knowledge of God, I failed to deal with my own pain. Instead, I poured my energy on everyone around me and their needs. I hid my pain well. Internally, I was dying, but on the outside everything appeared fine. No one would have ever known my history. At night my tears continued to stain my pillow.

As time went on, my husband was offered a job promotion out of state. As we prayerfully searched for God's direction, He made it clear this was His will. Although we did not understand it, we accepted the move, and before I could blink, moving trucks were in our driveway and we were on our way. The promotion allowed me to be at home. I used the time God had provided to seek Him. I was eager to find His will for my life. I wanted a ministry. I wanted to serve Him.

The gift of being at home also allowed me the time to reconcile with my dad. I learned his health was at serious risk. The emptiness his heart had carried from losing his family had caused him to resort to years of companionship with alcohol. With other health factors, as well, it was clear that if there was no change, his life could come to an end. As I heard this news, something clicked inside me. I did not want to lose my dad. I decided that if I did not extend the same grace God gave to me, my dad might never know God's grace.

I called my dad and could hear the pain in his voice. I made arrangements as soon as possible to go visit him. Once I arrived, I made appointments to consult with his doctors. My health profession knowledge gave me the skills to assist my dad in some medical changes. In just a few days with God's help we received a new doctor, insurance, and medication to assist my dad's recovery.

But the greatest achievement was the new relationship between me and my dad. His spirits were lifted as he discovered his daughter's love for him, and that was the best medicine of all.

Since this health scare, we talk on a regular basis and see each other when we can. Our conversations have brought me much joy. I thank God for the opportunity. We have been able to discuss issues of the past with much better understanding. Dad shared that after the loss of his family, his goal was to drink himself to death and die at an early age. We recently had a conversation where we both recalled his statement and agreed that God had different plans. I was thrilled to find out that we both share a passion for words and both have the talent to put them together in a meaningful way. Years had been lost, but new moments continue to mend us together.

I still pray daily for Dad because he still battles health issues, but I praise God as He continues to deliver him from Satan's alcohol trap. My Dad's health is better than it has been in years, and I am thankful God is allowing him time to share in the blessings of his family.

I began journaling more, writing devotionals and prayers. God urged me to write. He had a plan for my writings and I needed to seek His will. Through God's intervention, I found myself in a phone conversation with the president of Proverbs 31 Ministries. I shared with her the desires I felt God had placed in my heart about writing. She encouraged me to press forward and invited me to attend a writer's conference. She asked me to pray about a topic and put together a proposal to share. I accepted the invitation, chose a topic, and presented a proposal on godly step-parenting.

My heart was heavy on this subject because of the increase of divorce rates. The experience I had from my own broken family motivated me to want to place something on shelves to help parents equip their children to break this terrible chain. As I searched for supportive material, I was amazed at the small quantity for such a growing population. If parents cannot create a sense of worth in the home and build concrete families, our children will lack the crucial support needed to thrive or even survive society's cultural, educational, and economic systems. I titled it *Stepping into Motherhood*.

The writing conference took me on a spiritual high such as I had never felt before. I gained skills, made good friends, and overcame my fear of speaking. I also had the opportunity to present my proposal to an editor for Harvest House. Although the editor liked my proposal, it was not accepted. He encouraged me to continue working and make it unique by adding more of a personal testimony. Just the opportunity delighted me, and I learned writing was more about obedience than opportunity.

Writing was truly about experiencing God. Then something else happened during the weekend. God stirred my soul about the abortion. Something was not right. Why did I continue to relive this horrible day and carry this burden? I believe this was a pivotal turn for me. I believe this is when God began revealing my need and His will for me. In the midst of all the blessings I received over the weekend, two seeds were planted. First, the instruction to tell my personal testimony, and second, the examination of healing from the abortion. I was not sure what to do with either seed.

I returned home, and the busyness of life turned my weekend into a distant memory. Within three months I could barely put one foot in front of the other. Fatigue had taken over my body. The weight on my chest made it hard to breathe. I became concerned something was wrong physically. I made an appointment to see a doctor and put my mind at ease.

During my visit my blood pressure was 80/50. The doctor said I was severely depressed. The doctor recommended an antidepressant and gave me a hotline number to call if I felt suicidal. Suicidal! *How did I get to this point?* There was no way I would ever take my own life. I refused the antidepressant. I could not continue to try to conceive while taking the medication. The doctor felt my health was more important than trying to conceive and asked me to put pregnancy on hold. I refused. No one was going to tell me I had to put pregnancy on hold. I needed this. Did you catch that? At this point my want for a baby had become a need to overcome my loss from abortion.

I walked back to my car in a fog. I knew I needed help, but the help I wanted only came from above, not from a pill bottle. Despite my circumstances, I had grown enough in my faith to know God was bigger than any of this. I cried out for help. Instead of driving home, I drove to the Christian bookstore. I walked around again in a fog as I heard the staff say, "Can I help you?"

"No thanks," I replied. For goodness sake. I had no idea what I was looking for or why I was even there. I began to walk toward the door to leave when my eyes were drawn to a book titled *Get Out of That Pit*.

I knew after reading the first page that God wanted me to have this book. It was written to rescue souls from depression. Through Scripture the book identifies who is responsible for depression, how we become victims, and how we overcome the battle. I had cried out for help and God had answered. That afternoon, with my Bible in one hand and the book in another, I began to be delivered. I paced back and forth, quoting God's Word. At the time, we were living in an apartment so I am sure my neighbors thought I was crazy. They must have heard the Spirit releasing in me as I had "church" on the second floor of the building.

I had discovered I was depressed, but I still did not know the true source of my depression was coming from the abortion. I thought it was a combination of other stressors in my life. As a result of it all of it, I had lost my vision. I could not see a promised future because I was too busy living in the past and in my present circumstances. In the book I read, "There is no one on earth Satan would rather see in a pit than someone with godly vision."

Reading this made me furious. Satan had done this to me. I thought, *How dare Satan steal my identity?* I was not going to allow him to have victory over me. It was my choice and I wanted out of this pit. He may have pushed me in, but he could not hold me there. I was tired of living with no joy. I called out to God and He extended His grace once again and began helping me climb out. "He brought me up also out of a horrible pit, out of the miry clay, and set my feet upon a rock, and established my steps" (Psalm 40:2).

This is where I really began to let God work in my life. The climb out of depression did not happen overnight. It was a battle and I continued fighting it every day. Over time it affected my marriage. Men suffer the effect of abortion as well as women. In fact, my husband has given me permission to share with you some of his journaling during this fight for his marriage.

Here is what he wrote:

> Jeannie is struggling to balance her emotions. I know raising my two children from a previous marriage is not an easy task. As I watch her struggle with the inability for us to conceive, and the past abortion, I have come to realize that the most devastating part for her is the abortion. I have seen how it consumes her thoughts and is a part of her everyday life. The

frustration of dealing with the past abortion and her inability to conceive has caused her to become depressed. One day I came home and Jeannie was upset. She made a statement that chilled my soul. She stated, "I feel God has cursed me because I had an abortion and I may never have a child of my own." Behind the tears I saw terror and hurt. She sobbed in my arms like a little child. I didn't know how to respond. All I knew was we needed help. I continued to see depression and frustration battle to defeat Jeannie's loving kind spirit. All culminated into misery and psychological pain for her. I pray God gives us the solution to her pain and depression.

My husband realized that my depression was caused by my abortion before I did. God gave him spiritual lenses to look through so he could see my deepest needs and yes, God victoriously answered his prayer.

Chapter 5

The Awaited Invitation

MOVING TO ANOTHER state was quite an adjustment for me. I never realized how hard it would be. Most mornings, once my husband left for work and the children left for school, I lowered myself to the floor and sobbed. I felt so alone. I missed my friends, my family, but mostly the fellowship of my church. I never knew how hard it would be to find another church to call home. The search went on for nearly thirteen months until God led us to our destination. It was during those thirteen months that God planted us in the right service on the right day at the right church to receive an invitation.

We were running late as usual. I took a seat and the usher passed me a church bulletin. I held it tightly as I took my seat and participated in worship. During

47

announcements, I began to browse the bulletin. My eyes were drawn to a need for volunteers at the Piedmont Women's Center. I carefully tucked the bulletin away in my Bible. That evening at home, I pulled it out of my Bible. God would not let me lay it down. I sat at the computer to do some research and what I discovered was the Piedmont Women's Center was actually a pregnancy medical clinic caring for women with unplanned pregnancies. I didn't know much about this ministry, but I knew God wanted me there.

That same night I talked it over with Carter. He encouraged me to call the center and volunteer. Carter told me he thought volunteering at the center would help me heal from my pain. "Use your experience to help others," Carter said. He also encouraged me that this may be the ministry where God wanted to use me. As I listened to Carter's words, I thought about all my suffering, and it came to me there has never been a breakthrough of any kind without suffering. As Christians, we are going to suffer. If I did not suffer, how could I ever share my experience and give testimony of how God rescued me?

Romans 8:16-17 says, "The Spirit itself beareth witness with our spirit, we are the children of God: And if children, then heirs; heirs of God; and joint heirs with Christ; if so be we suffer with Him, we may be also glorified together." In 2 Timothy 1:8 (KJV) Paul tell us we are not to be ashamed of the testimony of our Lord, nor of ourselves as His prisoner: but "to be thou partaker of the afflictions of the gospel according to the power of God." What Paul is saying here is to be ready. Suffering is going to come and it may be difficult to share our faith, but God will give us strength and we can call on the Spirit to give us courage.

I spent the rest of the evening pondering how God could possibly use my pain to help others. The word that kept coming to my mind was grace. Then God led me to Acts 20:24, which reads, "But none of these things move me, neither count I my life dear unto myself, so I might finish my course with joy, and the ministry, which I have received of the Lord Jesus, to testify the gospel of the grace of God." So plainly put, my life is worth nothing unless I use it to finish the work assigned to me by the Lord. The decision was final. First thing in the morning, I was going to call.

The next day I phoned the Piedmont Women's Center and told them I wanted to be a volunteer and made an appointment to meet with a staff member. During our first meeting she asked me if I had ever had an abortion and I replied yes. As our interview continued, she discovered I had not received God's complete healing. She was so tender and encouraged me to take a post-abortion Bible study. She told me that once I completed the Bible study, I could volunteer at the center. I really wanted to volunteer so I accepted the invitation.

As I drove home, I couldn't help but wonder if she was right. In my mind, I battled the idea of taking the study. A part of me did not think I needed it. I knew God had forgiven me, but maybe there was more. Maybe I wasn't truly healed. I wondered if this was causing all the unhappiness in my life. Once I got home, I told Carter about the meeting, and without hesitation he encouraged me to take the study, so I agreed to try.

A couple of weeks later someone from the Piedmont Women's Center phoned me to schedule the Bible study. As she talked about the study, I still found it difficult to discuss the subject of abortion. She shared with me that she was post-abortion and she had also taken the study. Before our conversation ended I asked her, "Is this really going to help me?"

She replied, "Jeannie, it is the next best thing to salvation." I remembered how happy I was when I received Christ. I couldn't imagine anything better. If there was anything close to filling me with joy as salvation had, I wanted it. I enrolled in the Bible study and the dates were set. I drove with hesitation to the first Bible study. Satan was attacking my mind all the way. I am sure there was heavenly warfare taking place in my defense. I got lost on the way, and because I was running late I thought, *I should just go home.* I didn't want all eyes directed to me. I was nervous and fearful of judgment. Finally, the God of peace prevailed. One of the facilitators called and helped me find my way. I parked the car and walked inside.

The facilitators were so kind. As they greeted me at the door, I felt their love instantly and I felt more at ease. I found myself a seat in a circle of chairs. As the other attendees came in, I began to get nervous again. I found it hard to make eye contact with any of them. My mind reflected back to the day I sat in the waiting room with other girls waiting to abort. It seemed to be the same feeling of shame. When I finally urged myself to look around the room, I became aware of their nervousness as well. It was not a comfortable place for any of us to be so early in the morning. I was comforted knowing we all had something in common.

The facilitators prayed and some discussion began. They asked us to take a moment and find one word describing our life after the abortion. I immediately thought of the word "shattered." The definition of shattered is "to break suddenly into pieces as with a violent blow, damage seriously, disable, and to cause destruction." It was during this first session I truly realized just how much I was in need of a Savior. The shame had resurfaced. I no longer denied the fact I had been unsuccessful in turning off the feelings connected to my abortion. Up to this point, I still avoided any books, magazines, or commercials relating to abortion or babies.

In public I found myself looking the other way if I saw someone pregnant or someone with a baby. If I had to shop for a baby gift, I ordered it online so I would not have to enter the baby department of a store. It was more than I could stomach emotionally. Just hearing the word "abortion" caused shame to rise in me. Physically my heart skipped a beat, and sometimes I even held my breath.

God placed a precious circle of women in my path, who led me through this life-changing, post-abortion Bible study called *Forgiven and Set Free*. It was not an easy journey. In fact, I was broken into pieces as God rescued me from sixteen years of depression, anger, shame, and guilt. I came to know God in a whole new way as He became my personal Healer. He allowed me to lay my shattered life before Him to be redeemed. What a gift! He gave me a new life bursting with hope in exchange for my brokenness.

As I reflected on some questions during the study, I realized I was actually in pretty bad shape. I held resentment and unforgiveness in my heart, causing me to be a bitter woman. The questions made me dig deep enough to discover most of my personal struggles were stemming from the abortion. The emptiness and shame were still causing me to conceal my secret, and I was overwhelmed with the fear I would never be a mother. My self-esteem was damaged before the abortion. Afterward, it was destroyed. I struggled looking at my reflection. I repeated harmful patterns as a form of punishment. For example: I denied myself meals and developed an eating disorder.

The memories of the abortion were more painful than the actual experience. I was living in a constant state of loss. My journal exposes how the abortion affected me. "I am always trying to meet someone's approval. I want to be someone else because I don't want to face who I am. I feel distorted. Lord, I don't like Jeannie. I have no love for this person You created. Who is she? Lord, I seek healing in the area of self image."

I thought my self-image had been restored when I accepted Christ, but it had not. Much healing needed to take place. God began to give me vision to see my need. I did not know what the next several weeks would hold for me as I participated in the Bible study. Truthfully, I was scared so I clung to Genesis 50:20, "But as for you, you thought evil against me, but God meant it for good, to bring to pass, as it is this day, to save much people alive." I wrote in my journal and highlighted "as it is this day." I didn't know what was ahead, but I knew God was doing something brand new (see Isaiah 43:18-19).

When it is time, God will move on behalf of his children. The last entry I made in my journal asking God to free me of my abortion pain was more than four years ago. It wasn't until three years after that entry that He freed me—a little over one year ago today. Isn't that amazing? God has done so much work in such a short amount of time. It was the journey that equipped me.

During my three-year waiting period, God was equipping me. Supernatural things began pointing me to His plan. God influenced my mind, will, emotions, and body to desire what was pleasing to Him. He wrote His instructions on my heart so I would obey them (see Hebrews 8:10).

As the next Bible study session drew near, I prayed for peace. I felt God was urging me to press forward, but restlessness and uncertainty caused me to question the directions I had received. I submitted these concerns to God and continued to pray for peace. Confirmation came and so did peace. "Peace I give to you," He said, "let not your heart be troubled, nor let it be fearful."

As I prepared myself to take a step forward again into the unknown, God was encouraging me to obey by doing something that required trust and faith. God spoke only to be obeyed and in His perfect timing. He knew when I was ready and when He called, my response was immediate obedience. Is God urging you? What will your response be when He calls you? Position and prepare your heart to hear from Him.

Chapter 6

The Amazing Restoration

GOD WAS URGING me to trust Him. In order to fully trust Him with the deep pain of my abortion, I needed to understand His character. I began to study the names of God. As God revealed Himself through these names, I became more familiar with His nature. I had heard these names before, but this time it was on a more intimate level. Intimate because He was personally meeting my needs through His names.

I tried to narrow down one name to claim for my life. They were all so good. As I prayed, God revealed to me that His names meet specific needs. God directed me to the name Jehovah-Rapha which means "The Lord My Healer." I am tearful as I can recall the very moment He spoke to my heart and said, "Jeannie, I have come for you. I am yours. I am your Healer."

For me, there is no sweeter name than Jehovah-Rapha. As I called on His name, He cured me—restoring me emotionally, spiritually, and physically. As I list some other names for you, search your heart and decide who you need God to be to you. Then claim it and stamp His name on your life.

Jehovah-Jireh meaning The Lord my Provider.
—Genesis 22:14

Jehovah-Mephalti meaning The Lord my Deliverer.
—Psalm 18:2

Jehovah-Shalom meaning The Lord my Peace.
—Judges 6:24

Jehovah-Sali meaning The Lord my Rock.
—Psalm 18:2

Jehovah-Uzzi meaning The Lord my Strength.
—Psalm 28:7

Jehovah-El Emeth meaning The Lord God of Truth.
—Psalm 31:5

Jehovah-Maginnenu meaning The Lord my Defense.
—Psalm 89:18

Jehovah-Goelekh meaning The Lord my Redeemer.
—Isaiah 49:26, 60:16

Jehovah-Immeka meaning The Lord Is with You.
—Judges 6:12

There are three primary names of God in the Old Testament; God (Elohim), Lord (Jehovah), Master (Adonai). Beyond these, God is called by more than eighty other compound names or descriptive titles. Isn't that amazing? The God of the Universe chose to reveal His names to you and me. If I did not list a name that meets your need, search the Old Testament until you find the special name God desires you to call Him.

I realized during the study how bitter my heart was. I asked God to turn my bitterness into sweetness. I asked Him, "Please, Lord, show me what to do to be healed."

During my study of Scripture, I became aware God was a God who sees and a God who hears. I was able to relate my own life to the story of Hagar in Genesis 16:1-13. In this passage Hagar is running away from her problems. The angel of the Lord told her to turn around and face her problems—to submit to them and accept God's help. This would require a change in attitude, but God promised to multiply her seed for her obedience. Indeed, God blessed her. He heard her affliction and saw her need, so Hagar called Him "the God who sees me."

I related. I had spent years running away from the memory and sin of my abortion. Why was I running? I was wearing myself out from the run but getting nowhere. God was there with me when I had the abortion. He heard everything. He saw everything. There was no reason to run. He patiently waited until I stopped, turned around, and faced my problem. The moment I did, He was waiting with open arms to be my liberator.

I no longer had to hide anything. He knew my pain. He knew the deep, dark, shameful secrets of my heart (see Psalm 44:21). The God of the universe who created me regardless of my sin still loved me and He brought me comfort. I had not given God enough credit. When He said He was my Healer, He meant He was my Healer and it was time for me to respond. I started accepting God as my personal Savior. The knowledge I was gaining from the study was preparing me to receive His healing and apply it to my life.

No one knew of my participation in the study except for my mom, my husband Carter, and one dear friend. Carter and my friend encouraged me along, but Mom felt that continuing would be difficult for me. She didn't feel I needed to relive all the pain from my abortion. Her motherly instinct was protecting her child, and although I love her dearly for it, she couldn't have been more wrong. Reliving it was exactly what needed to happen.

I had to overcome my years of denial. What was I trying to hide by choosing abortion? I believe I was trying to hide my sin of having unwed sex. The other concerns I discussed in previous chapters were valid. Ultimately, I came to the conclusion I did not want to destroy my image. I sinned to cover up another sin. I was just hurting myself. Right? Wrong. I was hurting God. He was the one against whom I was sinning.

I realized my sexual impurities. I read 1 Corinthians 6:15 and was immediately convicted. This scripture may sound harsh, but sometimes the truth of God's Word is harsh. It reads, "Do you not know that your bodies are members of Christ? Shall I then take members of Christ, and make them the members of a harlot? God forbid." My body was God's temple and I had dishonored it.

God brought to mind each and every sexual sin I had encountered. I had been forgiven of these sins, but now it was important to heal from them. I asked God to purify me from my sexual sin. This was not an instant process, as God revealed every sexual memory from all my previous relationships. Individually, I recalled the sin and asked God to purify me from my sexual immorality.

Then I had to face the fact I had ended my unborn baby's life. This was the most difficult stage of my recovery, but it was necessary in order for me to accept the reality of my loss. Scripture showed me that the world had lied to me. My baby was not a mass of tissue. It was indeed a life that began at conception. Psalm 139:15-17 says that He creates every life from its earliest days in the womb. The earliest days are conception. He alone originates life (see Genesis 1:26-27). In Jeremiah 1:5 God says, "Before I formed you in the belly I knew you." God clearly makes the statement that He alone knits every life together and knows us even before we come forth from the womb. This strongly destroys the discussion of life beginning after exiting the womb.

As I recognized my baby's life, I began to grieve tremendously. The facilitators from the Bible study had given us a copy of human embryology to take home and review. God began revealing details to me. I was able to remember that it was cold outside when I had my abortion, so I determined it must have been in the late fall or winter months. The only other thing I had remembered was how far along I was in my pregnancy, which was about eight weeks.

That night as I studied the embryology of my baby, I was severely emotionally broken. The pain I endured was greater than the abortion itself. I learned that at eight weeks my baby could respond to touch and could feel pain. At eight weeks the organs and body systems are present. I was in agony, to say the least, knowing my baby could feel pain. My eyes locked on those words, and I began weeping like a child. I was crying so loud Carter came into the room. He found me lying on the floor wrapped in a blanket. The tears were coming so fast I was having difficulty getting my breath.

He scooped me up and said, "Jeannie, what is wrong?"

I showed him the handout and said to him "What kind of woman am I? I murdered my baby. I hurt my baby! Oh God! My baby could feel the pain." As I continued to cry, I was devastated to know my baby felt the pain of being ripped out of my womb. As Carter held me I began praying out to God. "Oh God, please, please I pray you spared my baby from feeling any pain."

I continued to pray this over and over, rocking back and forth just as I had on the day of my abortion. I was seeking comfort.

This was a very dramatic scene. The episode almost caused me to stop the study. I told Carter I couldn't continue. I couldn't bear it. He encouraged me to stick with the study and see it through. He said, "I know God has a plan and a purpose for your life." He asked me to call one of my facilitators and share my struggles with her. I agreed to do so.

As I talked to my facilitator, she explained to me this sorrow must take place in order for me to receive God's healing. She prayed with me and encouraged me, saying that once this journey was complete, I would be a new creature in Christ. Because she had walked a similar path, I believed her. Her beauty always lit up the room. I knew she was filled with joy, and I wanted what she had. I made the commitment to continue no matter how hard it got.

My husband helped carry my burden through this process. He too was committed to this recovery period. My pain had affected him and our marriage. At this point in the recovery, here is what Carter was able to write in his journal:

God has answered my prayers. Jeannie has been going through a Bible study for post-abortion women. The lessons are difficult for Jeannie due to the emotional content. She wanted to quit after the first few meetings. She stated she could not handle the memories of what happened. I encouraged her to continue. I know God is at work.

Lately she has seemed emotionally worse than before she started. She walks around in a bewildered state after the meetings, upset about the knowledge she is gaining. Sometimes she goes to bed early, crying herself to sleep. I want to rescue her, but I must step back and let God work. I know a lot of walls have to be broken down in order to build back a strong, happy, beautiful woman.

Wow! This supports why I stated that God brought the right man into my life to meet my needs. God gave him insight. I did not need Carter to rescue me. I needed God to rescue me.

As I drew close to God, I could feel His presence with me. Sometimes His presence was so strong and alive I felt I could reach out and touch Him. It was though He was sitting right across the room. He began to speak to me through scripture. When God shows me scripture I always date it in my Bible. Sometimes He will bring my attention back to the same scripture and I will date it again. When this happens, I pay close attention because I believe He is trying to tell me something.

On three different occasions dated 3-1-08, 1-25-09, and 2-8-10, He guided me to Exodus 19:5-6. It reads,

"Now therefore, if you will obey my voice indeed, and keep my covenant, then you will be a peculiar [special] treasure unto me above all people: for all the earth is mine and you shall be unto me a kingdom of priests, and an holy nation. These are the words which you shall speak unto the children of Israel."

Interesting enough, the last date listed was at the beginning of the Bible study. I didn't know what God was trying to say to me, other than He wanted me to obey. So I prayed and told God I would be obedient to whatever He called me to do.

As the lessons continued, I juggled everything else in my life. I still struggled with difficulties of conceiving and stayed in prayer about a child. My desire for a child was sometimes more than I could bear. Over the last year Carter and I became emotionally drained from fertility treatments. Our doctors came to the conclusion there was no reason the two of us could not conceive. It just was not happening. They encouraged us to explore other fertility options. As heartbreaking as it was, I knew God was not ready to give us our reward. I refused to continue with the fertility treatments and chose to wait on God. I felt I needed to put all my focus and energy into the study in order to fully receive my healing. It was not easy to let go of something I desperately wanted, but I trusted God's timing. I wanted to receive my blessing from Him and Him alone.

Once I came to grips with the fact my unborn baby was indeed a life, I asked God to make it more real for me. I asked God to give me more insight. I wanted to know if it was a boy or girl. I also asked Him to give me a name for him or her. I continued to try to remember more details from my abortion, but I lived so many years in denial and buried the memory so deep, the details were difficult to uncover.

My emotions were overflowing more at home. As much as I tried to hide them, I could see the children were concerned. One day as I was reading my Bible, God laid it heavily on my heart to share my story with the children. I said, "God, they are just children. This is too much for them to understand." But, honestly, what I feared more was destroying their image of me as their godly stepmother who had brought them to Christ. I was their role model. What would they think of me if they knew I had chosen abortion? I could not ignore God, so I submitted what I thought I heard back to Him. Then I heard, "You said you would obey. Do you not trust me? Will you not obey me now?"

Reluctantly, I got up and slowly walked into the room where the children were and shared my story. I explained my abortion and how God had brought me to this study to receive healing. I apologized for my behavior but told them it was necessary for me to recover from my pain. I sat trembling, waiting for their response. Suddenly, they both circled their arms around me and we all cried. No words from them were needed because I could see their hearts through their eyes. It was amazing. God had prepared them to hear from me. I now had the support of not only my husband, but also my family. I had made the mistake of doubting God.

In the next lesson, God began showing me I was full of anger. I never would have guessed this was an issue for me, but indeed it was. I did not know it was there—it was hidden and denied. As I searched the core of this bitterness, I discovered I was bitter with myself, but also with Mom. I was angry with her for not stopping me from having the abortion. I was angry with her for not discussing it more with me. I was angry because I felt alone in my decision. Untreated anger remained silent and caused bitterness to root in my heart.

Keep in mind that I did not realize the bitterness was there, so my relationship with my mom carried on as usual through the years. It was not until I began going through the healing process that Mom and I were able to talk about the abortion and I was able to share with her my feelings. I discovered the abortion had caused just as much pain to my mom as it did me, and she also carried regrets. After sixteen years, the two of us were finally able to talk about my abortion. That in itself was healing.

As we talked, Mom remembered something I did not. She told me my baby was due around my birthday, which was in August. This meant I got pregnant around November. Eight weeks later, when I had the abortion, would put the abortion somewhere in January, which made sense because I remembered the coldness outside. I was excited that I was gaining knowledge. I wanted every single detail to resurface. I felt this was the only way I could heal completely. I took a step further and called the clinic that performed my abortion to request a copy of my medical records.

I told my facilitator about the request for the records. She was shocked and told me she had never had an attendee do this. She encouraged me not to open the findings until the study was over. She felt it was vital to focus on the process of healing. I agreed this was the best thing. Shortly after, the records arrived. I stared at them in my hands. The return address made me cringe. As much as I wanted to open them, I kept my promise and placed them in a safe place until I was ready. I needed to continue my recovery.

I learned through an exercise provided by the study that I needed to forgive myself, my mom, the father of the baby, my friends who were involved, the doctor, and the clinic. I had to let go and forgive. It seemed like too big a mountain to climb, but really it was not. It was very simple. God forgave me and had mercy on me (see Psalm 86:5), therefore forgiveness was not an option. I too had to forgive. I was in no position not to forgive others.

The most difficult one to forgive was myself. I took my baby's life. But if I wholeheartedly did not forgive myself, I would be denying God's character and the truth of His Word. My choice not to forgive would also discount my witness of God's work in my life. This I refused to do. Forgiveness mirrors God.

I also needed to ask forgiveness for the pain I may have caused others, such as the baby's father. That did not require me to contact him. It was between me and God. I had to trust God to take care of the rest. The result of forgiveness brought me much peace. It was important to take care of this issue because unforgiveness hinders prayers (see 1 Peter 3:9-12), and I had much I wanted to ask God for.

Even though I had made much progress, I had to be careful not to let bitterness creep back in. This required me to stay on guard against Satan's attacks and to be spiritually prepared for battle. I had done so by memorizing scripture. Memorizing scripture also helped me fight depression. I have listed further scripture in the back of this book for your defense. You will find it listed by subjects. I encourage you to pick a scripture that addresses your struggle. Memorize a verse that will enable you to defeat attack when it arises. Notice, I did not say *if*, I said *when*. The Bible clearly tells us that trouble will come to all of us.

Satan continually used my desire for a child to try to reinstate my depression. Because of all my other obstacles, it was the hardest stage for me to overcome. It came and went. My depression was born when I took my grief, anger, and unforgiveness, and turned it inward. My depression was self-inflicted. I was able to overcome depression by also changing my thought process. When I felt negativity trying to take over, I tried to focus on all the positive things with which God had blessed me. If the attack was stronger than me, I cried out to God in my trouble and He saved me from distress (see Psalm 107:13). The Bible says God will bring you out of darkness and break your chains apart (see Psalm 107:14). God was doing just that. But I wanted to fully be delivered, so I made this request to God.

By now I was more than halfway through the study. I waited for my full deliverance to come. I was going away for a couple days to attend a conference for work. I was excited because all expenses were paid and my husband was going with me. At the last minute, my husband's schedule changed, preventing him from going. I was sad because I really wanted to spend some time with him. But as it turned out, God had other plans. He wanted me to spend time with Him and not my husband.

Once I checked into my hotel room and got settled in, I pulled my Bible out. I worked on some homework from my Bible study class. The peace and quiet was wonderful. I felt God's presence very strongly. I missed my husband, but I knew if he had been there the two of us would be out sightseeing, which meant I would not be in my room working on my study. Then I realized this trip was a gift from God. He had arranged it so the two of us would be absolutely alone. There had to be a purpose. I thought, *What is God doing?* As I meditated on this truth, I felt extremely special. I looked around the beautiful room given to me for my pleasure. Everything was perfect! For the first time since I pranced around the floor in my little girl pumps, I felt like a princess.

The next morning I went to class. I was thankful for the knowledge I was gaining to enhance my profession, but I was eager to return to my room and dive back into my studies. Finally 5:00 P.M. came and I headed back to my little paradise. Hunger struck. No problem, I thought, as I had been given a very generous food allowance. I scanned the room service menu. The meals looked exquisite. I was getting ready to order dinner when suddenly I felt God wooing me. I didn't want to miss a second with Him. The food could wait. His words are more necessary than food (see Job 23:12). I dropped the menu and went over to my Bible.

I wasn't sure what God wanted me to see, so I got facedown on the floor and started praying. I know what you must be thinking. Face down on a hotel floor. Yuck! But this is the posture I take when I am seeking God. He is pleased when we humble ourselves before Him. Don't misunderstand me. I am not saying you need to get on your face during your prayer time. You can come to God in any posture with a humble heart. This posture is what I personally choose to do.

Once I stopped praying, I sat up and reached for my Bible and notes from the study. I came across a scripture I had circled. Obviously it was a scripture one of the facilitators had given me, but I did not remember the content so I looked it up. I turned the pages with an eager and expectant heart. Finally, I reached Ezekiel 36:25. It was May of 2009. Sixteen years after my abortion and three months into the study when God said to me, "I will sprinkle clean water upon you, and you shall be clean." Tears started pouring from my eyes, but they felt as if they were pouring from my heart. I stared at the verse for a long time until God urged me to read on. There was more.

Still sitting on the floor, I read Ezekiel 36:26. "A new heart also will I give you, and a new spirit will I put within you: and I will take away the stony heart out of your flesh, and give you an heart of flesh." Something was happening. It was though my heart was being stripped—as if it was being torn down and rebuilt. I was weeping. I placed the scriptures across my heart and lay back on the floor and allowed God to perform His miracle. "And God shall wipe away all tears from their eyes and there shall be no more death, neither sorrow, nor crying, neither shall there be any more pain for the former things have passed away."

During this priceless occasion, He also revealed to me my unborn baby was a girl. He impressed upon my heart a name to give her. Another prayer answered. I had a daughter and her name was to be called Abagail, meaning "the Father's joy." The gift of giving her a name was just the beginning of the blessings I encountered in recognizing her life.

It was that night when God took something shattered and turned it into something beautiful. I am so glad I was obedient to what He wanted me to do because it was in that moment of obedience that God completely delivered me and healed me from my abortion pain. He knew the words I needed to hear from Him and He knew when I would be ready to receive them. Your words may be different. What makes the experience so supernatural is that when God meets *your* personal needs He becomes *your* personal Savior.

I am not sure how long I lay there, but when I finally got up, I knew I was a new woman . . . and I was starved. Feeling light as a feather, I pranced over and picked up the menu to order my dinner. After placing my order, I soaked in God's presence until there was a knock on the door.

"Room service." I opened the door to find a sparkling silver tray.

"Thank you," I said. I carried it to the table and unveiled my requested dinner of:

Rosemary Roasted Moroccan Lamb
Olive Oil Glazed Potatoes
Steamed Asparagus

Warm Roll with Butter
Spinach Salad with Cranberry Red Wine Sauce
Rum Raisin Bread Pudding with Pecan Carmel Sauce
Water and Sweet Tea

It was served on the most elegant, beautiful china. It was so good. I ate until my belly hurt. It was the most expensive meal I had ever had. I stayed awake as long as I could. I didn't want the night to end. I wanted it to last forever. When my eyelids wouldn't stay open any longer, I crawled into bed.

The next morning I got up refreshed and packed my suitcase. It was time to go home. As I made my way to the door, my heart was sad to leave such a special place. I turned around to take one more look at my little paradise, when God spoke to my heart and said, "My child, be uplifted. Your new heart leaves with you and so do I."

Once I got home I shared with Carter what had happened. We both rejoiced in answered prayer.

The next day I returned to work. My supervisor asked, "Did you have a good time, Jeannie?"

"The best," I replied as I placed my expenses on her desk and quickly exited the room. I am sure she was taken aback when she reviewed my meal receipt totaling seventy-five dollars. Ouch! A meal not only fit for a princess, but fit for a queen.

Chapter 7

The Breaking Free

TOWARD THE END of my healing, the greatest gift was the acceptance I was able to capture as I marveled at the life of my Abagail. This was essential to my healing. I acknowledged before man and God that my aborted baby was indeed real—a beautiful gift from above. With the support of my husband and children, we publically memorialized her death. This gave me the chance to celebrate her life.

One morning I decided to sit down and write her a letter. This was not an attempt to communicate with her. Scripture is very clear that communication with the dead is prohibited. This was simply a way to express my feelings on paper. In a moment of silence, I begin to write what my heart was longing to say to her.

Dear Abagail,

You and I were taken away from each other so long ago. It was such a confusing and lonely time. There were so many wounds in my life. Even before you, I was searching for ways to ease the pain of those wounds. I was so young with no guidance and next thing I knew there you were. Your presence made me more confused and scared, and I felt like I had nowhere to turn. I made a wrong choice to let you go.

I want to say to you that I am so sorry, my sweet one. On that cold winter day Mommy did not know what she was doing. For so long I have hurt and carried the burden of our bond being broken. I have imagined your beauty and wondered how you are. You will soon be sixteen and, oh, how I have missed you through the years. Somehow, I know if you could, you would let me know you miss me too and you are doing fine.

I dropped the pen. As the Spirit prompted me, I closed my eyes, peace filled my soul, and I imagined her reply.

Mom, you don't have to worry, be sad, or wonder if I hurt because on that cold day you made a wrong choice. . . . God was there. He took my tiny little hand and led me safely home. There is no pain here, no tears, so Mom it is okay. You have been forgiven and I will see you soon.

I know my leaving left such a void in your life, but God wants you to fill it with joys. Share our story and use it to save others like me. For those like you, teach them. Teach them as God taught you not to be burdened with sorrow, but to lift up your heart to Him and trade it for peace and the sunshine of tomorrow.

I wrote what I heard and, lastly, I promised Abagail I would bring purpose to her life. I then wrote a letter of thanks to God and placed them both in a beautiful keepsake box. It had been a three-month journey, but my healing was now fully complete. I cried out to God, thanking Him for what He had done. I told Him in exchange I wanted to offer my life to Him to use it in any way He chose to help others and bring glory to Him. I prayed, "Here I am, Lord, use me" and believe me, when you offer a willing heart, God will take full advantage of it.

I later learned of a place in Chattanooga, Tennessee, called The National Memorial Site for the Unborn. The history of the site intrigued me. The facility is dedicated to healing generations of pain associated with the loss of aborted children. Years ago, the site was an abortion clinic. Between the years of 1975-1993, 35,000 babies died on the premises.

The clinic opened a couple years after abortion was legalized. It was the only abortion clinic in Chattanooga. God used the mustard seed faith of area Christians to permanently close this facility. They gathered in the parking lot and prayed for salvation and for those ending lives to be removed. They prayed the site would be delivered into the hands of God's people. Consequently, in different seasons, both owners developed cancer and died.

After years of obedient prayer, God provided the opportunity and means to purchase the property and evict abortionists. In May 1993, the last abortion was performed and the clinic was closed. The building was gutted and remodeled, and the land was dedicated to the glory of God. Chattanooga is now one of the largest cities in the United States without an abortion clinic.

In 1994, the grounds became a place to honor the unborn and seek the Lord's forgiveness. A couple years later the Wall of Names was created. It is a fifty-foot granite wall that holds small brass plates with words of remembrance put there by mothers, fathers, and other family members from all over the nation. When I learned of this wall, I took full advantage of it.

I was honored to hang my Abagail's nameplate on the wall, referring to the scripture John 8:36, "Indeed we are free." The same nameplate is framed and rests on the mantle in our home. It is important to me that she remains an active part of our family.

The site also has an area dedicated to the memory of children lost to miscarriage. It is open twenty-four hours a day. I recommend its use for further healing and a way to honor your child's life. After you donate a plate to the wall, by Internet you can visit and virtually tour right to your nameplate for a visit. What a blessing! Dr. James Dobson's comment on the site was "What a victory!"

My family and I are traveling there this summer to celebrate Abagail's seventeenth birthday. God continues to bless. It brings me much joy to share with you what God has done for me, and what He can do for you also. Of course, I still live with the regret of my abortion. As I continue to desire another child, I have to wear the armor of God and remind myself that I walk by faith not by sight (2 Corinthians 5:7). Through it all, I would not give up the journey. It has been the journey God used to change my life forever.

I finally reached my destination as a volunteer at Piedmont Women's Center, and God is indeed using me there. I work as a counselor for women facing unplanned pregnancies. Most days I see myself in their eyes, and each day I walk into the clinic, I am given the opportunity to share my story and save lives. What an awesome privilege. Praise God! You see, I am living proof that God works all things for good (see Romans 8:28).

I opened this book with Isaiah 61:1-3. I chose this scripture because God first chose it for me. I desperately asked God to reveal my purpose. I asked, *What is my ministry? What do You want me to do with the writing desire You have given me? What do You want me to write about?*

I am one of those stubborn gals who has to be shown over and over again. Thankfully, God did not lose patience with me as I kept asking the same questions. Over a period of several months, God continued to bring me to Isaiah 61. It was right before my eyes, and I finally got it. This was my purpose. This was my ministry. God called me to gather the brokenhearted from abortion and lead them to freedom.

There were so many other scriptures God used to direct my path. There are too many to name here but interestingly enough, they all confirmed I was chosen to speak and write His truth. He then revealed that I should write about abortion. Finally, it made sense. All the other assignments were just to prepare me for this big one. He was equipping me, but I still did not know how this was all going to take place.

I drew close to God. I knew He was at work. The very next day after I noted the scriptures in my journal, God began to put the project of this book into play. He directed my every step. Within hours, God had placed me in contact with the right publishing company. They were thrilled about the title and accepted my proposal. This was an extraordinary move from God and a day I will *never* forget. I cried off and on for hours as I soaked in His presence and joy.

Later that evening, I was hungry to spend more time with God. I marveled at His movement in my life. As I read His Word, He directed me back to Isaiah 61. I snickered and thought, *I got it God; I know what You want me to do.* But there was something more He wanted me to see. He directed my eyes further down to verse 7. It read: "For your shame you shall have double." At that moment everything in time stopped. I melted in my seat. Tears began to stream. God's Word was very clear and very promising. For my shame, God was going to give me double. I can't wait to see what double is, but I sure hope it's twins! Many times God has returned me to verse 7. Magnificently enough, it is always when my heart is heavy for a child. It is His gift of assurance. He is so sweet.

When it was time, my obedience brought to presence the desire of my heart to write for God in a mighty way. As I reflected on my life, I saw God's footprints all over it. He was knitting me together piece by piece.

I recently gave a friend a birthday card that read, "You are His masterpiece." As she read it, she stated, "A masterpiece? No one has ever called me a masterpiece," but indeed she is because I could see God at work in her life. Each and every one of us is His own unique masterpiece. What will you look like when He is done with you?

A couple of weeks after I finalized the book project, I got a call from my director at Piedmont Women Center where I counsel. She asked if I would share my testimony at a banquet for life. I hesitated because speaking in public is not my favorite thing to do. I told her I would pray about it. After I hung the phone up, God instantly reminded me of my words to Him. "Here I am—use me." He also reminded me of the scriptures He had given me. He instructed me to speak. I thought to myself, *Yes, Lord, where You lead I will follow.*

I called my husband, Carter, and told him about my hesitancy to share my testimony. He encouraged me to press forth and not to give up an opportunity to share what God had done for me. I agreed and immediately called my director back and accepted the invitation to speak at the banquet. She then asked me to call the coordinator of the banquet to discuss the itinerary. The coordinator was thrilled of my acceptance. Towards the end of our conversation, she asked if my husband could also speak and share how my abortion affected his life and marriage. I could not wait to call my husband back to tell him the good news. When he answered the phone I said, "Carter, they want you to speak at the banquet too!" He replied, "Wait a minute!" I laughed. It seemed he was not as excited to speak himself as he was for me.

It is important we recognize the pain men also endure from abortion. Carter's voice needed to be heard to bring forth hope for the fathers. For every hurting mother there is also a hurting father who has lost a child because of an abortion decision. For these fathers I suggest participation in a Bible study for healing and hope. I have made some recommendations in the resource section of the book.

Two days later, my husband and I both spoke at the banquet and gave witness to God's loving grace and healing. As I waited to speak, I held tightly in my hand a rock given to me by one of my facilitators at the end of the Bible study. Written on the rock was 1 Samuel 7:12-13. The rock was my "Ebenezer" and symbolized deliverance and a reminder, "The Lord has helped us."

As we were introduced as speakers, I gripped my rock and we made our way to the stage. As I walked to the podium, tears filled my eyes. I thought of His miracle. God took me, a young woman filled with shame, a woman not able to talk to anyone about my abortion, and turned me into a woman of courage who was able to stand in front of hundreds and give testimony of His love and healing. My obedience brought forth amazing blessings that night. Doors of healing opened.

Millions of women around us are still hurting, still grieving, from their own abortions. I recognize you. You are wives, daughters, neighbors, friends, coworkers, even women with whom we worship. Many are looking for healing. God has provided. May His Word reach the world!

Chapter 8

The Ugly Truth

I HAVE BEEN called to one of the most influential and significant ministries of our time. While the issues of our nation's economy dominate the headlines, I can't help instead to shift my thoughts to the three babies who die every minute because of abortion. Nearly every twenty seconds there is an abortion death, which means there are over 4,000 a day. How heartbreaking is that fact? One in every three women will have an abortion by the age of forty-five, and a startlingly seventy-eight percent of women who have aborted report a religious affiliation. Think about that. Next time you attend church, glance down the pew where you sit. Based on these statistics, one in every fourth woman sitting there has had an abortion.

In the world, 1.3 million abortions are performed yearly. In the United States alone, over 48 million unborn babies have been killed in the thirty-seven years since abortion was legalized in 1973. This legalization was done only one year prior to my own birth. This means that during most of our nation's history, abortion was forbidden as the unjust taking of innocent life. Now, fifty-four countries allow abortion, which is about sixty-one percent of the world's population. So how did we get to this point? What happened to us as a nation? To whom is the world listening?

My answer to the questions is that as a world we have decided to take things into our own hands. Our shipwrecked faith causes us to do what is right in our own eyes. We have decided that only *we* know what is best for our lives. We have decided *we* have the right to choose. We have decided it is better to base decisions on feelings and circumstances than on truth. Boy, have we got it all wrong! We have left out the most important part of the equation—God. Simply put, we have turned away.

The world argues that life begins after birth. However, from the earliest days of creation, God says life begins by Him in the womb. He originates it and created us in His own image (see Genesis 1:26-27). The world says we have the right to end life. God says it is not your life to take, for "I am the Beginning and the End" (Revelation 22:13). In brilliant fashion, God shows the origination of life in the very first chapter of the Bible, and then reveals He alone is the end in the very last chapter.

Abortion is an extremely private matter. It takes courage for any woman to talk about the details of an abortion. There are very few safe moments with only a few people when we are given the opportunity to speak freely. It seems not many want to hear about a woman's experience with abortion unless they have gone through it themselves. It is a subject many want to avoid because it's uncomfortable. Unfortunately, most women remain silent because of their fear of judgment.

I remained silent for years because of my own fear of judgment from family, church, peers, pretty much everyone around me. Remaining silent caused my imprisonment and led to years of shame and guilt. It was no fun walking around, impersonating a fraud. It was not until I spoke it and released it that my freedom began.

It will not always be an easy challenge. I still sometimes get shunned because of my ministry, and sadly sometimes it even happens within church walls. We live in a generation where judgment overflows in our churches. All we can do is pray that God changes hearts.

I encourage you to be silent no more. I am not saying to run through your neighborhood and tell everyone; that is, of course, unless you want to. Share with the ones you need to share with. You know who they are. It is your story alone. With God's discernment, pick and choose with whom to share this sacred testimony.

Please hear me on this. You will never completely heal until truth is revealed. It has to resurface and be brought to the light in order for the destruction to be torn down. This is imperative in order for God to restore and rebuild a strong, healthy heart.

Here is the true story of one woman who chose to be silent no more. When I read her story, I froze in my chair as my heart broke from her experience. I have written a portion of it here for you.

> I was called in to witness and assist with an abortion. I had never seen an abortion. My job was to hold the probe on the woman's abdomen. I could see the full profile of the thirteen-week-old baby from head to toe. As the probe came closer to the baby, I could see the baby trying to move away from the probe as if it was trying to find safety in its mother's womb. The baby was fighting for its life.

This woman was the director of a Planned Parenthood abortion clinic. She resigned after seeing the procedure that day and now fights for the rights of the preborn. She states, "I realized everything I had been told by Planned Parenthood was a lie." Thank God she was asked to take part in the procedure so her eyes could see the destruction and her voice could be heard.

At thirteen weeks this baby was well-developed. As you continue to read, I will give you insight into fetal development at this age and what kind of procedure must have been performed.

This woman was a Christian who went to church every Sunday and truly believed she was helping women make better choices. She states, "My biggest regret is coercing women into having an abortion." I believe there are still individuals like her today who are unaware and who continue to play a role in abortion clinics. If it had not been for my own unawareness at the time of my abortion, I would have a hard time believing anyone could be so blinded by Satan. But believe me, it happens.

Abortion clinics are trained to sell abortion. Abortion has become a gluttonous income. The money is not in family planning or prevention, it is in abortion. I recently viewed a picture of proceeds from one business day in the clinic. The picture was an oversized trash bag overflowing with lifeless babies. I literally felt I was going to vomit. How corrupted!

When God appointed the time, I reviewed the medical records I had requested from the clinic where I was treated. I was accurate in my calculations. I had become pregnant in late fall and the abortion date was in January, eight weeks into my pregnancy. As I reviewed the charts, I was overtaken by a statement signed by the performing physician. It read: "I am the attending physician for the above patient. Upon review of her chart, and after discussion with her, I am of the opinion that the risk of her physical and/or mental health which would exist if this pregnancy were to be continued is greater than the risk of an immediate interruption of pregnancy by vacuum aspiration."

The paperwork continues to show the findings of my baby girl, Abagail, and describes her not as a baby whose heart is completely formed, but as products of conception. It identifies all her fetal parts present as thirty grams of spongy, firm, red tissue.

I thank God for the strength He bestowed upon me as I read these records. I share this with you because it is important that you know there never was a discussion between the physician and me. The anguish and pain I have endured from the abortion physically and mentally are far greater than any struggle or fear I could have encountered raising my child.

I was angry when I read the records. The physician's statement was a lie and an act taken to cover his actions and/or the clinic's. My physical and mental health were in no danger because of my pregnancy, but rather have been damaged because of my loss. Discovering this ignited me even more to devote my life to taking a stand against abortion. I attempted to take action against this physician, but I was told he was deceased. My courage to share my story comes from my desire for you to use my testimony as backbone to seek justice and, most importantly, to save lives!

When a woman considering abortion is confronted with proof of life, she is more likely to choose life. This can be accomplished by providing a prenatal ultrasound. I have witnessed the saving of many lives from the encouragement of this procedure. I do not want there to be any misunderstanding on fetal development. If you are facing a decision regarding your own pregnancy, I want to immerse you in this truth before you decide. If you are post-abortion, it is important you recognize the development and life of your baby at the time of your abortion.

Stages of Fetal Development

Days/Weeks	Outcome by Development
Day 1-4:	Conception takes place. The baby's features, including sex, hair, and eye color is determined.
Days 5-9:	Developing baby, now an embryo, implants in the uterus.
Day 21: (3 weeks)	Human heartbeat starts
4-5 weeks:	Heartbeat becomes more regular and stronger and begins circulating baby's own blood. Eyes and ears form, fingers can be seen, organs are identifiable, arms and legs begin to appear.
6-7 weeks:	Brain waves can be recorded, baby responds to movement, family traits are evident, muscles are forming, baby can kick, swim, and suck his or her thumb.

Days/Weeks	Outcome by Development
8-9 weeks:	Nervous system is functioning, heart is completely formed, baby can respond to touch and can feel pain. (This is typically the time frame when abortion clinics want to perform procedure)
10-11 weeks:	Baby can make sounds and can swallow
12-16 weeks:	Sex clearly identifiable, movements are felt by mother
17-24 weeks:	Lungs are developing, baby has hair, hiccups often, has the sleeping patterns of an infant, hears everything adults can, permanent teeth buds form behind milk teeth.
25-36 weeks:	Baby has grown to fill the full available space, legs are now in fetal position, baby develops immunities, continues to mature until birth.

I also find it vital that abortion procedures be understood. There are five major methods. They include:

Manual Vacuum Aspiration: Surgical abortion done within seven weeks. A hand-held syringe is attached to tubing that is inserted into the uterus and the baby is suctioned out.

Suction Curettage: This is the most common. It is performed within six to fourteen weeks. Tubing is inserted into the uterus and connects to a suction machine. The suction pulls the baby's body apart and out of the uterus. In this method, a loop-shaped knife is sometimes used to scrape the fetal parts out of the uterus.

Dilation and Evacuation (D&E): Performed thirteen to twenty-four weeks. The body of the baby is too large at this time to be broken up and pass through suction tubing. Because of this, a dilator must be inserted a day or two before the procedure. After opening the cervix, the doctor pulls out the fetal parts with forceps. The baby's skull is crushed to ease removal.

Dilation and Extraction (D&X): This procedure takes three days and occurs from twenty weeks to full term. During the first two days, the cervix is dilated. On the third day, medication is given to start labor. After labor begins, ultrasound is used to locate the baby's legs. Grasping a leg with forceps, the doctor delivers the baby up to the baby's head. Next, scissors are inserted into the base of the skull to create an opening. A suction catheter is placed into the opening to remove the skull contents. The skull collapses and the baby is removed.

RU 486 (Abortion Pill): This is used for women who are within thirty to forty-nine days of pregnancy. This procedure requires three doctor visits. On the first, the woman is given pills to cause the death of the embryo. Two days later, if the abortion has not occurred, she is given a second drug that causes cramps to expel the embryo. The last visit is to determine if the procedure has been completed.

There are also risks to consider such as infection, drug reaction, damaged cervix, scarring of the uterine lining, perforation of the uterus, damage to internal organs, breast cancer, and even death. In addition to these risks, abortion can reduce your ability for future conception.

I know this material is harsh, but I cannot sugar coat the details of abortion. The word "death" brings discomfort. Why? Because we were created to live eternally and whether we want to admit it or not, each sweet baby who loses his or her life to abortion is living eternally with Jesus their Creator.

Recently someone asked me, "Wouldn't abortion be okay in a case where there was an indication for special needs like Down syndrome or cerebral palsy?" My reply was, "Abortion is never okay; for any indications. It is murder." I continued to explain that God has a purpose for each and every one of us, whether we live a full life or not. Our hairs are counted, and our days are numbered by Him alone.

There are always options. If a teen determines she cannot raise a child, or if the pregnancy occurs unwillingly, opt to give the baby up for adoption. There are plenty of couples eager to become parents. Choose life. If there is an indication for special needs, God will provide the resources and support you need. Love covers all circumstances. There is no scenario you can give me that justifies ending life through abortion.

I often wonder what my Abagail would have accomplished. I wonder what her career and ministry would have been. God had a plan for her life that she was not able to fulfill because of abortion. Knowing this has broken my heart many times—and that brings me right back to the heart of this book.

Our time together is drawing to an end. I know you are broken from your loss, and I wonder if I have reached your heart yet. I surely hope so. I pray your heart is mended by God's everlasting truth, grace, and love. Let God be the keeper of your soul. Let Him be your deliverer. Be not ashamed. Be not afraid. Put your trust in Him.

I assumed this chapter would be one of the easier ones to write. However, I was wrong; it has been the hardest. I wholeheartedly believe I encountered spiritual warfare while preparing and writing this chapter. I felt it was important to deliver the content of this chapter because if it had been delivered to me, my choice would have been different. Satan absolutely fought to keep the information I just shared with you concealed, but God is victorious. With His help, I was able to come to completion with every detail He wanted written.

> As for you, you thought evil against me; but God meant it for good, to bring to pass, as it is this day, to save many lives.
>
> —Genesis 50:20

Chapter 9

The Final Question

RECENTLY I APPROACHED a sales clerk at the bookstore. "May I help you?" she asked. "Can you please show me everything you have in the store on the subject of abortion?" I replied. As I stood at the counter awaiting her reply, I could not help but notice how many heads dropped when I said the word abortion. I was haunted as to what caused their heads to drop. Only God knows. Interestingly enough, the sales clerk could not produce much material on the subject.

I am convinced there is a world out there in desperate need of healing. As I left the store, I carried my head high in thanksgiving to my sweet Savior. There was a time not long ago when I too would have hung my head at the sound of the word, but now I can boldly speak it.

This chapter is dear to me. It is the sole purpose of this book. I have taken you on a journey through my life and shared with you my deepest thoughts and secrets so that Christ can rescue you. God is eager to make a covenant with your heart so that He may be your God and you shall be His people (see Jeremiah 31:33).

It was not nails but our sins that held Him to the cross. It was our wrath that put Him there. He lovingly bore the pain and shed His precious blood so we would not have to carry sin. If you choose to carry it then you deny who Christ is and what He has done for you. He says from the least of you to the greatest of you, I will forgive your iniquity and I will remember your sin no more (see Jeremiah 31:34). It is only by His mercy that we are not consumed. His faithfulness, mercy, and compassion is new every morning (Jeremiah 31:33). There is no way we can ever thank Him enough for what He has done for you and for me.

This time has been elected for you to self reflect. My final question to you is this: **Are you truly healed?** I prayerfully chose the following questions as a tool for you to discover your answer. Some of the same questions were given to me and opened my eyes to recognize my own need. My request is that you be honest as you answer these questions, and my prayer is though you were once blind, now you can see. "Let us draw near with a true heart in full assurance of faith, having our hearts sprinkled from an evil conscience, and our bodies washed with pure water" (Hebrews 10:22).

Are you unable to talk about your abortion?

Have you experienced long seasons of depression?

Do you deny feelings connected to your abortion?

Do you live in denial that it ever happened?

Are you affected by physical reminders such as other babies, baby clothes, pregnant women, sound of a vacuum?

Do you desire pregnancy again in hopes of replacing the aborted baby?

Have you experienced any self-destructive behaviors?

Have you experienced any flashbacks or nightmares associated with the abortion?

Do you fear you will never be able to have children again?

Are your emotions numb?

Do you feel sad or depressed on the anniversary date of the abortion or the anniversary of the due date?

Are you haunted by guilt or shame?

Are you struggling with forgiving yourself or others involved with the abortion?

Are you overprotective or is there a failure to bond with any living children?

Do you fear God's punishment?

Do you feel unworthy?

Do you experience self-hatred?

Do you have unexplainable crying spells?

Do you suffer from bitterness and anger?
Do you feel alone, isolated, or rejected?
Do you have marital stress?
Do you tolerate abusive relationships?
Do you have difficulty with intimacy?
Do you have alcohol or drug addiction?
Do you ever think of suicide?
Do you find it difficult to find joy in normal sources
      of pleasure?

In the beginning, I answered yes to many of these questions. If you also answered yes, you too could be experiencing post-abortion stress. You cannot overcome it on your own. You need the touch of the Master's hand. Seek participation in a post-abortion Bible study. It is important you are surrounded by others who share your need, understand your need, and can support your need.

You will be facing issues and feelings you may have avoided for a long time. You will probably feel vulnerable and insecure—which is what makes the support of the group so important. It will be difficult, but trust me; you do not want to miss out on the journey and the blessings on the other side. It will be well worth it. There will be tears, but God will wipe them from your eyes and there will be no more crying or pain (see Revelation 21:4). Your lips will shout for joy as you sing praises to Him who has redeemed you (see Psalm 71:23).

I was once given an invitation that changed my life. Now I would like to offer you the same invitation. Join

The Final Question

God in His plan. He has made the resources available to you. If you are post-abortion and continue to carry your burden, this book was written for you. It is no accident or coincidence that you are reading it. It is a part of His plan. My heart aches for your freedom. You are invited to receive His powerful healing. This invitation does not expire, but why delay the results? He is waiting for your reply.

> Come to me those who are weary for I am the Lord that healeth thee.
>
> —Exodus 15:26

From the Author

Dear Friends,

I FIND MYSELF thinking of you and am thankful for the love God has given me for each of you. You are women of all races, ages, backgrounds, different hair colors, different eye colors all beautiful by God's design. It is no mistake that we come from different walks in life, but one thing remains true; we were created by a loving God who calls us His own. I pray you have clearly been able to see God's footprints and the blessings he has bestowed.

There are many of you who will not have the courage to share your abortion and seek recovery publically, but maybe you are reading this in the privacy of your home and you are ready to lay your past down at His feet. In either event, I am steadily praying each and every woman bearing the pain of abortion will be delivered. You do not have to carry the burden of who you've been because you are forgiven. At times it may seem that He is far away. On the contrary, God pays close attention to those who call on Him. He wants nothing more than to save a crushed spirit (Psalm 34:18).

The journey will not be easy, but do not back down. God will continuously be present to hold your hand. When He is done, there is no greater satisfaction than discovering your purpose and daily fulfilling it. I have listed a bountiful supply of great resources for you at the end of the book. It would bless me tremendously to hear from you and how God is working in your life. I have provided my contact information below. I will be waiting for you. I am expecting great things. This is my prayer for you:

Father, Healer of my soul,

If we have ever needed You, it is now. You hold this world You created in Your hands and You see each and every tear that falls. Give the brokenhearted courage to come to the cross. Call them out; turn them away from guilt and shame. I ask that You take this body of shattered souls and turn them into beauty. Grow them, strengthen them, and do not stop Your work until these lives demonstrate Your heart's desire. Lord, we seek Your face and we know that our greatest days are before us and not behind us. We look forward to the miracles You have in store for us in Jesus' Holy name, Amen.

From the Author

Now, Let us lay aside every weight, and the sin which doth so easily beset us, and let us run with patience the race that is set before us, Looking unto Jesus the author and finisher of our faith; who for the joy that was set before Him endured the cross, despising the shame, and is set down at the right hand of the throne of God.

—Hebrews 12:1-2 KJV

My assignment is complete. My Father is proud.

In His Healing Love,

Jeannie

jeanniesmith.authorweblog.com

And they defeated him by the blood of the Lamb, and by their testimony, and they did not love their lives so much that they were afraid to die.

—Revelation 12:11 NLT

For Men...From Carter...

JEANNIE WAS INSISTENT that God wanted me to insert this addendum to the book. This is my testimony on how abortion affects a man, marriage, and relationships. I remember the day we were married and how beautiful Jeannie was in her wedding dress. When she arrived at the altar, the glow and beauty caused me to become overwhelmed with emotion. Little did we know that a few years later a situation with pain and depression would almost tear our relationship apart. The difficult situation was caused by an abortion that Jeannie had nine years prior to meeting me. In the beginning, prior to the abortion ever becoming a recognized part of the problem, there were underlying difficulties in our marriage relationship stemming from the abortion. Neither Jeannie nor I ever thought an abortion could cause this much emotional destruction. As our relationship grew, I began to realize that most of the emotional and mental problems with Jeannie were due to the abortion. The first subtle hint was the growing obsession with having a child. The disappointment every month when she realized she wasn't pregnant. She would sit and cry about her inability to get pregnant. This was a struggle for me. I felt helpless in the entire situation. Every month there was enough blame to go around for the both of us. I'm a firm believer that God is in control and His purpose is always at work. How do you share that with a grieving woman who desperately wants a child? I searched for ways to fix Jeannie and our marriage. As men we tend not to say the right things; we just look for ways to "fix it." This would cause Jeannie to become overwhelmed with sadness. She continuously would say, "I need someone to talk to. Someone who understands." She stated she could not talk to me. I just didn't understand. She was right. I was fixing and not listening.

Every day I could see the misery and pain on Jeannie's face. It was hard to explain…I would see her when she thought no one was looking. The grimace and anguish on her face was as if her arm was being twisted. She was so very miserable. Her outward appearance began to slowly decline. This was noticeable by her hair always up in a pony tail and decreased use of make-up. Of course, I began to believe all this was because she was unhappy with becoming an instant mother and wife.

Jeannie had taken on a lot by marring me and becoming the mother of two children from my previous marriage.

This began to weigh heavily on our relationship. I would dread coming home in the evenings from work. A man's home is supposed to be his haven, his place of peace. My home was neither. I never knew exactly which Jeannie I would encounter. Sometimes she would be nurturing and loving, but the majority of the time she would be angry and bitter. This unpredictable attitude destroyed the closeness in our relationship, and I also became bitter and angry. This brought tension into our relationship with each other and the children. We began to grow apart as husband and wife and as a family.

As our relationship continued to fall apart, we looked for avenues of escape from the reality of life. Jeannie would flee to our bedroom walk-in closet. I found her in this closet many times, sitting on our foot stool, sobbing like a child. I would find escape in video games and television. I would spend hours playing video games every night. I wanted to make sure Jeannie was fast asleep before I came to bed, to avoid any discussion.

Her anger and misery became replaced by depression. I tried to dismiss the idea that something was seriously wrong with my wife. She insisted on blaming me for the depression and pain. I was at a loss. So I did what any man would do. I withdrew into my own world. I avoided confrontation with her. I began developing a passive attitude with my family and friends.

I decided our life together could not stand much more of this abuse from either one of us. Our children, who we tried so hard to raise in a godly home, began to see the despair in our relationship. God even used the children to help bring reason to us as we spiraled downward out of control. Looking back now, the situation with Jeannie had caused me to become depressed. I felt my leadership in the home as a man began to weaken. How could I have let this get so out of hand? Broken and desperate, I began to pray and beg the Lord to help me. I prayed for a solution. I needed to give it to Jesus and pray healing would take place.

This was the point Jeannie mentioned the post-abortion Bible study. Jeannie began the study only to become more distraught and upset. Little did I know that God had answered my prayer. The post-abortion Bible study was the beginning of healing for Jeannie. It was a difficult journey for both of us. Jeannie had to unpack all the years of emotional pain and suffering so God could provide the forgiveness to set her free. As I watched her struggle, I felt so helpless and useless but humbled at the same time. I would hold her and pray silently for her.

I had to step back and let God complete his healing of Jeannie. When this occurred I began to see positive change in Jeannie with each Bible lesson. God had given her confidence back through the study. She began to let her hair down, the makeup came back on, and she began to have a glow about her. God had given me back my beautiful wife! All praise and glory to God for working a miracle in our lives and in our marriage.

It has been no surprise to me that God would call my wife to this ministry. I have watched as He has drawn her closer and closer to His will. I knew God would use her grief to help others and bring glory to His name. It has, however, been a surprise to me that God would choose to give me the opportunity to speak to the wounded hearts of men. Jeannie and I have been overwhelmed by the need for God's restoration in marriages caused by abortion. We find it humbling yet an honor to be God's example. It is our desire to lead other couples to receive God's healing in their marriages.

My brothers, has your life or marriage been affected by abortion? Encourage your wife to find a post-abortion

Bible study in your area. If you are the father of an aborted child, you too need to be involved in a support group and post-abortion Bible study for men. There is hope. No matter the brokenness and mistakes made throughout our lives, Jesus Christ is the only solution. Do not let pride, guilt, and shame hinder you, your wife, or your marriage from being forgiven and set free!

—Carter

Resources to Healing

Men and Abortion Network
www.menandabortion.net

Abortion Changes You
www.abortionchangesyou.com

The National Memorial for the Unborn
6230 Vance Road
Chattanooga, TN 37421
423-899-1677; 800-505-5565
www.memorialfortheunborn.org
www.rememberingtheunborn.org

Silent No More
www.SilentNoMoreAwareness.org

Piedmont Women's Center
Abortion recovery assistance
ara@piedmontwomenscenter.org
864-244-1434

Hope After Abortion
Hopeafterabortion.com

Healing Hearts Ministries
Online emotional support
www.HealingHearts.org
888-792-8282
253-268-0348

Fatherhood Forever Foundation
www.fatherhoodforever.org

After Abortion National Helpline
866-482-LIFE

SUGGESTED POST-ABORTION BIBLE STUDIES

Forgiven and Set Free
A post-abortion Bible study for women
By Linda Cochrane

Healing a Father's Heart
A post-abortion Bible study for men
By Linda Cochrane

Resources to Healing

Suggested Books

Brokenness
By Nancy Leigh DeMoss

I'll Hold You in Heaven
By Jack Hayford

Empty Arms
By Wendy Williams & Ann Caldwell

You're Not Alone
By Jennifer O'Neill

A Jewel in His Crown
By Priscilla Shirer

Get Out of That Pit
By Beth Moore

Breaking Free
By Beth Moore

Battlefield of the Mind
By Joyce Meyer

Her Choice to Heal
By Sydna Masse

A Season to Heal
By Luci Freed

OPTIONS FOR CRISIS PREGNANCIES

Bethany Christian Services
www.bethany.org
1-800-BETHANY
24-hour nationwide pregnancy line

Piedmont Women's Center
www.piedmontwomenscenter.org
864-244-1434
800-395-HELP
24-hour hopeline

Carenet
www.care-net.org
www.optionline.org
800-395-4357

Heartbeat International
www.heartbeatinternational.org
888-550-7577

The Nurturing Network
www.nurturingnetwork.org
509-493-4026

SUGGESTED SCRIPTURE READING

Where to find help when you are:

Resources to Healing

Depressed
Matthew 11:28-30; Romans 8:28; Philippians 4:13;
Psalm 107:14-15; Psalm 55:22; Psalm 34:19;
Psalm 9:9; 2 Samuel 22:29.

Angry
Matthew 5:22-24; Romans 12:10-21; Ephesians 4:26,
31-32; James 1:19-20; Hebrews 12:15.

Anxious
Matthew 6:25-34; Philippians 1:21; Luke 12:22, 25,
31; 1 Peter 5:7.

Bitter
Matthew 6:14-15; Romans 12:14, 17-19;
Ephesians 4:31-32; Hebrews 12:14-15; 1 Peter 2:23.

Hopeless
Romans 15:13; Colossians 1:3-5, 27; 2
Thessalonians 2:16-17; Hebrews 11:1.

Withholding Forgiveness
Matthew 6:14-15; 18:21-22; Mark 11:25;
Luke 6:37-38; 11:4; Ephesians 4:32; Colossians 3:13.

Suffering
Matthew 5:10-12; John 15:18-20; Romans 8:35-39;
James 1:12; Revelation 2:10; 2 Corinthians 12:10.

Discouraged

Romans 8:28; Galatians 6:9; Philippians 1:6; 4:6-7, 19; Hebrews 10:35-36; 1 Thessalonians 3:3.

Doubting

Philippians 1:6; James 1:6; 1 John 5:13; Hebrews 11:6; 12:2; 2 Timothy 1:12; John 6:37; Matthew 8:26.

Fearful

John 14:27; 2 Timothy 1:7; Hebrews 13:6; 1 John 4:18; Psalm 27:1, 91; 56:4; 118:6; Joshua 1:9; Genesis 26:24; Numbers 21:34; Deuteronomy 1:21; 3:22; 31:6; 31:8; Isaiah 41:10; 41:13; 1 Samuel 7:12-13.

Bibliography

Angelfire.com. (n.d.). *Children of Divorce: The Effects on Children of Divorce.* Retrieved July 2010, from www.angelfire.com: http://www.angelfire.com/rant/childrenofdivorce1/

Care Net. (2008). *Before You Decide: An Abortion Education Resource.* Care Net.

Care Net. (2009). *Serving with Care and Integrity: A Training Resource for Pregnancy Center Volunteers.* Lansdowne: Care Net.

Focus on the Family. (2010, January 8). *Former Planned Parenthood.* Retrieved August 2010, from citizenlink.com: http://www.citizenlink.com/?s=Abby+Johnson

Garcia, S. (2001, July). *Post Abortion: Regrets of Women Who Had an Abortion.* Retrieved March 27, 2010, from www.gargaro.com: http://www.gargaro.com/regrets.html

Guttmacher Institute. (n.d.). *An Overview of Abortion in the United States.* Retrieved August 2010, from www.guttmacher.org: http://www.guttmacher.org/media/presskits/2005/06/28/abortionoverview.html

Moore, B. (2007). *Get Out of That Pit: Straight Talk about God's Deliverance.* Nashville, Tennesse: Integrity Publishers, Inc.

National Memorial for the Unborn. (2010). *Our History.* Retrieved June 2010, from www.memorialfortheunborn.org: http://www.memorialfortheunborn.org/tabid/54/default.aspx

Rotenberry, R. L. (n.d.). *Names of God.* Retrieved July 2010, from lillyofthevalleyva.com: http://www.lillyofthevalleyva.com/jesuslovesyou-godnames-complist.html

Tyndale House Publishers. (2004). *Holy Bible* (New Living Translation 2nd ed.). Wheaton, Illnois: Tydale House Publisher, Inc.

Tyndale House Publishers. (1998). *Holy Bible: King James Version.* Wheaton, Illinois: Tyndale House Publishers, Inc.

World Abortion Statistics. (2006, November 3). Retrieved June 2010, from abortionfacts.com: http://www.abortionfacts.com/statistics/world_statistics.asp

Yates, A. (2002). www.homewithgod.com. Retrieved April 9, 2010, from *Home with God*: http:/www.homewithgod.com/cards/selfimage.shtml

WinePressPublishing
Great Books, Defined.

To order additional copies of this book call:
1-877-421-READ (7323)
or please visit our website at
www.WinePressbooks.com

If you enjoyed this quality custom-published book,
drop by our website for more books and information.

www.winepresspublishing.com
"Your partner in custom publishing."

LaVergne, TN USA
19 March 2011
220760LV00001B/1/P